ELEMENTARY ECONOMICS FROM
THE HIGHER STANDPOINT

ELEMENTARY ECONOMICS FROM THE HIGHER STANDPOINT

R. M. GOODWIN

Reader in Economics
University of Cambridge

CAMBRIDGE

AT THE UNIVERSITY PRESS

1970

Published by the Syndics of the Cambridge University Press
Bentley House, 200 Euston Road, London N.W.1
American Branch: 32 East 57th Street, New York, N.Y.10022

Library of Congress Catalogue Card Number: 72-116842

Standard Book Number: 521 07923 3

Printed in Great Britain
at the University Printing House, Cambridge
(Brooke Crutchley, University Printer)

CONTENTS

CONTENTS

PREFACE

The nature and shortcomings of this book are best explained by its origin; it is a rewriting of a course of lectures on economic principles to second-year undergraduates, given in 1967–68. The course had to be non-mathematical, for the general student; it was intended to cover only basic concepts with some of their broad implications, applied theory being left for separate treatment. The aim was to provide familiarity with some of the analytical tools needed by the present day economist.

A great deal of contemporary analysis appears in a form which effectively screens it from the majority of students, which, even if unavoidable, is also unfortunate. Feeling free of the necessity to encompass the whole range of principles, I decided to attempt to make some of the newer types of analysis intelligible to the non-mathematician. The shape of the book is dominated by this aim. It has always seemed to me that geometry is the proper way to bridge this gap in communication, and, indeed, it has largely been so since Marshall introduced the standard curves of economics. The diagrams, however, need bringing up to date, to cope with problems that our predecessors knew about but evaded.

The range of contemporary analysis is broad, but at least three types of problem stand out: global behaviour, interaction of the parts, dynamics. Much progress has been made in removing the inadequacies of received doctrine on these points. Although recent contributions are often strikingly new, they have a way of leading back to basic issues that concerned earlier economists. Thus general equilibrium was fully stated by Walras but remained an empty box until the work of von Neumann and of Leontief. Or again the accumulation of capital has been a tool and a trap for countless economists, but Ramsey recast the whole problem in a lucid and fruitful way.

The method I have tried to use is to formulate an ideal world, analogous to the real world only in its most important aspects, so simple that it is relatively easily and fully comprehensible. Throughout the analysis is limited to a two sector model, thus allowing the sense of some difficult, essential concepts to be grasped. Once these notions are understood it becomes possible to elaborate, with increased realism, the model in various directions. A few tentative steps are taken in Ch. 6; the attentive reader should try his own efforts at others. By stating clearly the assumptions made, I hope to emphasize some of the pitfalls on the path to economic reality.

The book is intended as a guide for the perplexed through a part of the weird and wonderful world of modern economic analysis. There is an abundance of such books and I have, therefore, felt free from any obligation to complete coverage. The trouble with guide books is that they tend to repeat previous ones, usually in a rather debased form. This one is, I fear, no exception since it deals with subjects dealt with countless times before. In an effort to minimize this anaesthetic effect, I have consulted no other books during its composition nor littered its pages with references to sources. This may explain, though it can scarcely excuse, its errors and omissions.

This absence of references to sources is not to be taken as indicating lack of them, but as expressing a feeling that all the analysis in this book springs from a body of doctrine common to most contemporary economists. Anyone interested in the intellectual origins of the work, will find more sources in my teachers than in my erratic and scanty reading. Particularly to be mentioned are Schumpeter, Leontief, LeCorbeiller, and Joan Robinson, who have all, each in a very different way, had a strong influence on my thinking, though never quite to the point of emulation.

Peterhouse, Cambridge   R. M. GOODWIN
April 1970

1

INTRODUCTION

1.1. Methodology

The peculiarity of economics is that everything depends on everything else, or at least on a number of other things. By contrast a falling body may be studied in complete isolation from almost everything except gravity. It is this structure of interdependence which gives the study of economics many of its peculiarities and its many traps for the unwary. An immediate consequence is that if we state our problems in all their completeness, they become, for practical purposes, insoluble, not in principle but simply because they are too complicated.

There is really no completely satisfactory resolution; any method has its gains and disadvantages. Marshall developed the *cet. par.* approach, which handles the bits and pieces well, but loses the drift of the whole, or worse still, may be positively misleading. By contrast Keynes dealt with aggregates which allowed him to treat the whole of the economy, but only by some rather rough handling of the parts. An alternative way out is to take an economy so simple that we may analyse the functioning of the parts and yet see how, by this mutual conditioning, they generate the behaviour of the whole. A price has to be paid for the gains: no very useful practical conclusions can be drawn, but it could be added that a lot of the apparent practicality of economic principles is spurious. Rather the aim is going to be to elucidate the how and why of some basic concepts, with attention drawn to various pitfalls in their use. No mathematics will be used but to take its place there will be extensive reliance on graphical analysis. Being therefore restricted to two dimensions, only two goods, the minimum necessary to show interdependence, will be dealt with. The basic concepts applicable to the more complex reality of many goods will usually apply to the simple case of two goods, where their nature is clearer and easier to grasp. The converse is less valid, but I have tried to keep to propositions which do carry over to the case of many goods. Another reason for treating an extremely simple economy is that, as is now generally recognized, it is essential to introduce dynamics from the start. Because this introduces considerable additional complications, it has been customary to restrict discussion to the case of one good (aggregates) but by extending ourselves to two goods we do get the essential element of interdependence without unbearable difficulties first. The aim of an economy is, or should be, to satisfy so far as is possible the desires of its members. This vision of the sovereign consumer reigning over the turbulent productive apparatus is likely to mislead to unwary. In fact, most of the crucial decisions shaping the economic structure occur in the productive sphere, e.g. what shall be produced, how produced, at what price, and most important of all, how much each consumer is given to spend on consumption. The poor fellow can still claim that he alone determines how he spends it, but even this is being seriously eroded in our advertising-ridden society. In any case we begin with the problem of production, and indeed, give only a brief and simplified treatment of consumption.

1.2. Constant costs and the production function

Throughout we shall be making the simplifying assumption that both goods are produced under conditions of constant costs. Although it is certainly not universally valid, it is perhaps more so than any other single, simple hypothesis, and it has obvious attractions as a powerful analytic tool. A plausibility argument for it may be taken from the theory of competition. When a firm has excessive profits, new firms enter with the same costs and gradually bring price and profits down. But what other firms can do can be done as well (or better) by existing firms. Therefore they can expand output indefinitely at existing cost level, if necessary by duplicating existing plants, complete with managers. There may of course be decreasing cost by enlarging the size of the plant, but this possibility must be over-looked in the interest of simplicity. From a technical point of view, the firm, then becomes irrelevant; the industry has constant costs regardless of scale and it does not matter whether this is by variation in size or number of plants or of firms.

These two industries, say α and β, each have one or more techniques of producing goods α and β, a technique is specified by the quantities of goods needed to produce a given output, and, in order to keep full generality, we assume each sector uses some of its own output as input. Constant costs means that for any one technique, doubling output requires doubling inputs, one-tenth one-tenth and so on for any quantity.

Hence if we have inputs used for any one output, we have them for all outputs; divide the input of, say β, by the output of α to find input of β per unit of output α. This input coefficient is multiplied by any level of output to find the required input. There are various techniques known and each will have a different set of input coefficients. The collection of all the sets of coefficients yields the production function of the industry (more properly the plant, but if all plants are alike then the difference disappears), because it gives all the production possibilities with known technology. This is a discrete production function with some limited number of techniques but nothing in between, and in some ways is more comprehensible than its more elegant twin, the continuous production function, where we imagine an unlimited number of techniques filling the spaces in between, so that we may find techniques using the inputs in any proportion. However, by combining any pair of techniques in various proportions, the stretch between them can be filled. Such a function, discrete or continuous, is linear and homogeneous; linear because all inputs and outputs are proportional, instead of, say, going by squares or square roots, and homogeneous because, no matter what proportion of inputs, we have the same constant proportionality rule for outputs. This function type, first used by Wicksell in economics and used and misused by countless economists since, is very convenient, in particular because it separates scale and proportion in production, an enormous convenience, as well become evident.

The same process is now applied to β, giving for unit output the inputs of β and of α for each known technique, the collection of these techniques constituting the discrete production function for β. All the coefficients for both α and β represent the complete technology of the economy and they may be arranged systematically as column of coefficients for each technique for each industry in turn, thus, for example,

α			β	
0·3	0·2	0·1	0·15	0·05
0·6	0·9	1·5	0·2	0·4

This rectangle of coefficients is the technology matrix of the economy. Suppose on historical or national grounds one technique has actually been chosen for use in production in each industry, we then get a Leontief input–output coefficient matrix, e.g.

	α	β
α	0·2	0·15
β	0·9	0·25

If we apply to the coefficients of each column the prospective output of the sectors, we get the inputs required, which are at the same time outputs required in the corresponding row. Thus, if we are producing 100 units of β there will be derived from this a demand for 15 units of α. These inter-firm flows are commonly cancelled out in economic analysis, but it has always been a dubious procedure and becomes increasingly so with the growing technical complexity of our productive mechanism. In order to avoid algebra and keep to simple geometry, our analysis will be restricted to two sectors, but it is easy to see how the model can be extended to any numbers of sectors by increasing the number of rows with the number of goods, and having as many columns for each sector as there are techniques. The analysis increases in complexity very rapidly with the increase in the number of sectors, but there is no qualitative change in the kind of problems or in the character of the answers.

1.3 Vectors

For graphical analysis of production the most convenient tool is the vector. A vector is a directed line segment, thus having the two aspects of length and direction. In terms of coordinate axes it is specified by its two components, i.e. its vertical projection on the two axes as shown in fig. 1.1. Its length is always positive, indicated by the arrowhead, in the positive direction of the axes. They are added head to tail, preserving length and direction but not position. Calling the first two α techniques, a_1 and a_2, we may represent them as vectors in fig. 1.1. Thus for all vectors (indicated by bold face) the production of one unit of α by a_1 inputs are given by its components, and if by a_2 by its components. Producing two units of α, one by each technique, will require inputs given by the components of $a_1 + a_2$ as shown. A vector may be multiplied by an ordinary number, i.e. a scale factor or scalar. This multiplies the length in that proportion. Thus if we produce 1·5 units by a_1

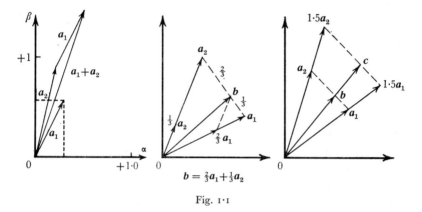

Fig. 1·1

its length is increased by 50 % and if we produce 2/3 unit its length is reduced by 1/3. From these two techniques alone we can arrange to use any pair of inputs in the area enclosed by a linear extension of the two vectors to infinity. One particular combination is important: suppose we wish to produce one unit of α, but we do not care how much is produced by each technique. What combinations of inputs will do this? As suggested by fig. 1.1 any input along a straight line connecting a_1 and a_2 will give inputs which will produce unit output, as a little experimentation will show. Not only this but the line will be divided by the point in the same proportion that we are using the two techniques. Now suppose we wish to use inputs in this proportion but that we wish to use 50 % more of both inputs. Multiply a_1 by 1·5 and a_2 the same and divide the line connecting them (fig. 1.1) in the same proportion, then c will equal 1·5 b. Thus we are able neatly to separate scale and proportion in any such problem.

The only other operation needed is the scalar or dot product, written $a_1 \cdot a_2$. As the name suggests it is not a vector but rather an ordinary number like length. It can be found by taking the vertical projection of a_1 on a_2 and multiplying it by the length of a_2, or equivalently the projection of a_2 on a_1 times the length of a_1. Reality requires n-dimensional abstract economic spaces not, alas, presentable visually. Alternatively, it is calculated by

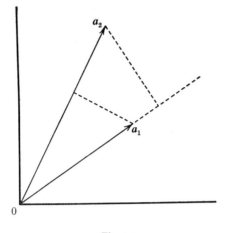

Fig. 1.2

multiplying the respective components of a_1 and a_2 and adding the result. A little experimentation will quickly demonstrate that the two methods give the same result. All these operation can be carried out for n-dimensional abstract spaces and provide the natural approach to the complexities of the real economic world of many goods.

1.4 Sectoral production

For the present assume that there are no unproduced inputs, labour being taken as unproduced. Take one of the goods, say 1, and consider it as produced by inputs of goods 1 and 2 (or any number of goods), a typical problem of the vectorial nature of economics. A complex quantity, say 3 bushels of wheat and $\frac{1}{10}$ ton of fertilizer produces a scalar output of, say, 20 bushels of wheat. It could be a vector output (joint product) say 1 wheat and $\frac{1}{5}$ fertilizer, but this is ruled out in the interest of simplicity. There is no direct way of comparing inputs with output, of saying whether it is a desirable thing to do, or, more important, how desirable in comparison with other known production possibilities. To make

6

these complex quantities comparable we need prices, and this is the meaning of prices and valuation, the explanation of the rather peculiar role of prices in an economy.

An economy is characterized by prices and quantities, p's and q's, and they constitute its fundamental duality. But they are not symmetric or parallel entities at all. There is no question but that the quantities of inputs and outputs produced with them are more basic, and that we can, and do, discuss, and, in principle, solve the whole economic problem without mentioning prices. By contrast a world of prices with no output would be an absurdity. Yet the role of prices is crucial in that they are the means by which the complexes of quantities are reduced to single scalar form and hence made comparable, and hence allow of simple decision making. For this reason, discussion of prices, though less essential, comes first.

By applying prices to inputs we get money costs and these can be added to get total unit cost, a scalar, and this can be compared with price to get value added by manufacture. Thus prices simplify a process and make it meaningfully comparable with others. These money values are obtained from the scalar or dot product of the price vector and the input vector, since it is the sum of the product of the components of the two vectors. The various combinations of inputs, which will produce unit output of good 1, completely specifies the technology of good 1 in conditions of constant cost. The producer faces some given set of prices, the price vector p. In fig. 1.3 the cost per unit output by process a_2 will be the length of its projection on p times the length of p (i.e. $a_2 \cdot p$). If we take p to have unit length, this cost is simply the length of the projection of a_2 on p, ob. The producers lay out this amount, ob, and get back p_1 per unit, or the projection of p on the unit output vector, e, for q_1 (origin to the point $+1$ on the q_1 axis), which is the same as the projection of this unit vector on p, oc. They lay out ob in money value and get back oc, so that the value added by manufacture is bc, a scalar. Prices have thus enabled one to get rid of the complication of vector quantities. Since there are no payments to unproduced inputs, the value added is also the surplus or profit per unit. Thus in this unrealistically simplified model, if we sum on all industry the value added by each, we get net national product which is equal to total profits.

7

Though such a situation could never arise in practice, it is a direct consequence of the assumption of no unproduced, valuable inputs. If the line from a_2 to ob be continued to d, it is evident that d divides oe in the same proportions as b does oc. ob/oc yields cost as a proportion of revenue and so does od/oe. But oe = 1, so od gives cost as a fraction of value, and oe less od gives profit as a fraction

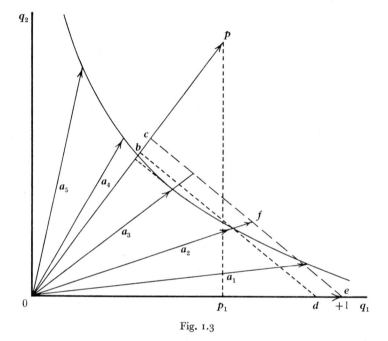

Fig. 1.3

of value. This profit rate, $\lambda = de/oe$, is for unit output, but it will be the same for 1 or 1 million units hence it is independent of the scale of output. It is likewise independent of the scale or level of prices, since lengthening or shortening p will increase or decrease the two scalar products in the same projection, leaving their ratio, λ, unaffected. This is the justification for using any particular length, e.g. unity, for p.

This profit rate which is often the more convenient, is, unfortunately, not the one used in commercial practice, and for good reason. The producer invests his input costs and reckons profit rate as profit divided by cost, not by revenue. Thus the conventional profit rate is $\pi = de/od$ whereas $\lambda = de/oe$. Since od = $1 - \lambda$, $\pi = \lambda/(1-\lambda)$ and $\lambda = \pi/(1+\pi)$. For small π, the two will be approximately equal, but if we buy for 2 and sell for 4, $\pi = 100\%$ and $\lambda = 50\%$. If a producer borrows money at a rate r for a time equal to his production period and repays at the end with interest, then we may ask what is the greatest rate he will be willing to pay —it is that rate which raises cost to price and reduces profit to zero, i.e. $(1+r)\ ob = oc$, or $(1+r)\ od = oe$ or $r\ (od) = oe - od = de$, and $r = de/od = \pi$. Thus his profit rate may be interpreted as rate of return on cost or rate of interest, thus

$$(1 +r)\ \boldsymbol{a_2} = (1 + \pi)\ \boldsymbol{a_2} = \boldsymbol{f}.$$

Now we can easily see which technique a producer will choose if he wishes to maximize his profit rate given $\boldsymbol{p}$. He will push the normal (perpendicular) to $\boldsymbol{p}$ as far towards the origin as possible so long as it still leads to a technique, $\boldsymbol{a_3}$ in this case. Cost is minimized and profit is maximized, the one being the bottom of a bowl, the other its reverse side, the top of a dome. This will maximize both π and λ for any scale of output. It is to be noted that he will only use one process for one good, whether there are discrete or continuous processes.

Now consider the scale of output. For any given technique, e.g. $\boldsymbol{a_3}$, we have the inputs required to produce 1 unit of output. With constant costs, increasing these inputs in the same proportion, say by 10 %, will increase output in the same proportion. If we add $g\boldsymbol{a_4}$ to $\boldsymbol{a_4}$, we get an output of $1 +g$ units at a cost of inputs given by the projection of $(1 +g)\ \boldsymbol{a_4}$ on the respective axes. Thus g acts exactly like π on $\boldsymbol{a}$ and is directly comparable with π (both are pure numbers) but its meaning is quite different. For π we have unit output and find by what fraction we have to increase cost to equal revenue. In the other we have some given quantities available as inputs and find by what fraction we can increase output to equal those physical inputs. This is in simple form one aspect of a fact von Neumann turned to such extraordinary use (see below, section 2. 5). To find the net result of operation of each of these techniques at unit output level, we need a slightly different construction (fig. 1.4). The output is a vector $\boldsymbol{e}$ of unit length along the q_1 axis. The usage of the two goods is represented by, for example, $-\boldsymbol{a_2}$ which is a vector of the length of $\boldsymbol{a_2}$ but in the opposite direction. Gross output is $\boldsymbol{e}$ and net output is $\boldsymbol{e} - \boldsymbol{a_2} = \boldsymbol{u_2}$. There will be one $\boldsymbol{u}$ for each process and the $\boldsymbol{u}$'s trace out the same curve as the a's did before but reflected and inverted about the q_1 axis. These a's will have the same projection as before on p except that they will be differently placed. Thus the cost per unit of producing by a_2 is $ob - oc$ and the profit per unit is oc. Thus the

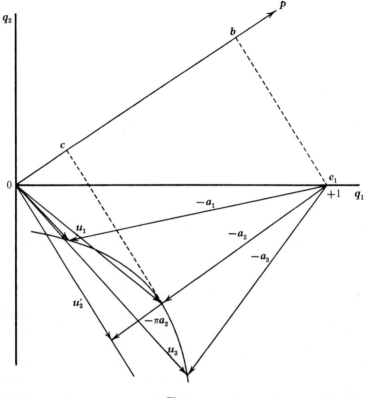

Fig. 1.4

dot product $u_2 \cdot p = oc$ is the profit per unit, i.e. the projection of net output on p. To find the rate of profit on any technique we must find that rate of interest, $r = \pi$, which will increase cost, including interest cost, to equal price, thus reducing profit to zero. Net product after interest cost is given by $u_2' = -a_2 - \pi a_2$, and the value of this, i.e. profit, is its projection on p. Therefore for $u_2' \cdot p$ to be equal to zero it must be perpendicular (or normal) to p. To find the rate of profit on any technique we find what portion of its a is required to extend a to the perpendicular from p.

2

CHOICE OF TECHNIQUE AND DETERMINATION OF RELATIVE PRICES—TWO SECTORS, NO FACTORS

2.1 Assumptions

Until they are explicitly relaxed the following assumptions hold: a closed economy, no durable goods, no technical progress, constant cost production functions, two sectors or industries, each producing a single homogeneous good. There are two types of inputs, produced and unproduced (e.g. equipment and natural resources); the unproduced ones are called factors. Throughout Chrs. 2 and 3, it is assumed that there are no factors of production, in particular no labour. This does not mean no labour or natural resources are used but that, like air, they are plentiful, have a zero price and hence may be ignored.

2.2 The price mechanism as computer

The economic problem is to determine how much of each good is produced, both net and gross, by what methods, at what price it is sold, and what profit and net income results. For a two-good economy this does not represent too complicated a problem and can be solved completely, say by economic planners.

But when there is a complex economy with thousands of goods, it becomes so complicated as to be unsolvable in practice. Yet the problem is solved, crudely and inaccurately no doubt but still solved, every day in the markets of the real world. How can this impossibly difficult task be accomplished, even imperfectly? The secret lies in the price-market mechanism whereby it is only necessary for producers to know the available technological processes for one good, plus the prices of inputs and of the output. Thus prices and markets may be regarded as an extraordinary, and very ancient, computational device of remarkable power. The market mechanism is a computer of a very special sort; it could be called a 'human-link analogue computer', i.e. it is an actual mechanism more or less analogous to the abstract mathematical economic problem posed above, and embodying human beings amongst its linkages. The price system is a way of simplifying the information needed in resolving the economic problem. The basic character of an economy is interdependence—no decision can be made for one part without relating it to all the other parts— yet this is just what prices do allow the producers to do.

2.3 Types of dynamic adjustments

The best way to understand the price mechanism is to simulate, albeit in a crude way, the actual adaptive processes of markets. This both reveals the character of any equilibrium (stationary, or unchanging) solution and gives some insight into the processes of change to which the economy is constantly subjected. It is the method, invented by Walras, of *tâtonnement* or trial-and-error solution of the economic problem. The name chosen by Walras is felicitous, through ominous; it refers to the search, by tapping, of a blind man for a goal, through a world, neither of which he can perceive.

Many different types of dynamic adjustment have been studied and it makes a great deal of difference—which one or ones are operative. Consider a four-fold classificaton of types. In the first type producers are price setters and when profit rates are different, they alter prices so as to bring the rates into line. From a traditional point of view this sounds very unreal, but in recent times it has found considerable favour in the form of mark-up in cost-plus price determination. It is especially useful in the description of the inflationary process and we shall use it here because it is the simplest mechanism. Next we have that, if output is greater than demand, output is curtailed and if less than demand, it is expanded. Disequilibrium implies variation of stocks and the explanation of inventory behaviour is perhaps the best performance of dynamics to date. The third type (especially used by Walras and the relevant to the short run) is a mixture of the first two: prices rather than output rise or fall as supply is less than or greater than demand. The fourth one (the particular province of Marshall and requiring a longer time) assumes that if profit rates are different, output will vary so as to bring them back into line. Since the last two are not contradictory, there is logically a fifth which may call cross-field dynamics, profit differences lead to output changes, discrepancies between supply and demand to alterations of price which brings us back to the profits with which we recommence the round.

2.4. Mark-up

It is a remarkable fact that we can determine market prices and the most profitable techniques of production without any reference to demand or output. This is of course, a direct consequence of the assumption of constant costs since no variation of output can effect cost or price and hence effect that industry or any other in its profit calculations.

We begin with primitive chaos; nothing is known except the various techniques for producing each good. No producer can state a price because he does not known his costs (which requires others' prices). In this unhistorical situation someone must choose at random a set, or vector, of prices and with these we begin. But here a difficulty appears, each producer must know in advance the 'right' mark-up, i.e. that which all will have at the end of the process.† This difficulty can be met by imagining a capital market which puts an interest rate cost lying somewhere between the highest and lowest mark-ups. Each mark-up rate is then adjusted so as to cover total costs including interest cost. Since there are no durable goods, choice of technique is completely free each period and there are no carryovers from goods purchased the preceding period (a problem which bothered Walras).

2.5 The determination of prices and techniques

To exhibit this process of tâtonnement repeat fig. 1.4 but add the same cost vectors for industry 2 radiating from its unit output vector e_2, as in fig. 2.1. Take any initial, positive, unit price vector p' and draw a line perpendicular to it through the origin.

† It can be shown, however, that even if all producers use any arbitrary common mark-up, they will end up with a common rate of inflation or deflation which applied to the money rate of profit, the mark-up, will yield the correct real common, mark-up rate of profit.

Each producer will then select his highest profit technique and this determines his profit rate, π, and hence his operative mark-up. These two profit rates will not be the same. Suppose that this capital market, supplying funds to both, sets the rate of interest in between

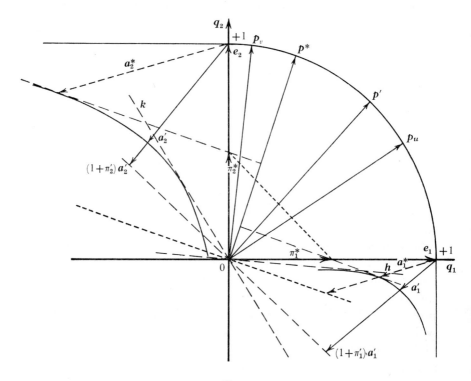

Fig. 2.1

the two profit rates, so that one will earn a 'pure' profit after interest cost and the other a negative pure profit, a loss. Using the chosen technique, each producer now sets a new price by marking up materials cost by the interest rate ('full cost' in this model) thus establishing a new set of prices with a common-mark up (the rate of interest). The new price vector can be found by extending the $\boldsymbol{a}$'s in a common proportion π''. They now earn the same operating profit rate but because of changed input prices, neither is maximizing his profit rate. So they now choose a new technique $\boldsymbol{a}''$ which can be found by finding the point on the unit isoquant whose tangent is perpendicular to $\boldsymbol{p}''$. But profit rates, equal at the previous tech-

14

nique, will no longer be so and a new market rate of interest (and hence mark-up) is established in between the two. This serves to set two further prices, p'''. This adjustment process continues and, for convex unit isoquants (convex set of techniques), will converge to a price vector which yields equal profits, at least cost, to each. It is not the best technique or set of prices for either, for there are prices which yield higher profit rates for either one separately, but there is no pair of techniques and prices which would yield higher profit for *both*. If we take p near e_1, π_1 will be near unity and π_2 correspondingly small. As p is rotated π_1 will decrease continually

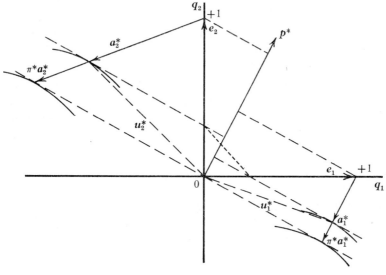

Fig. 2.2

to near zero and π_2 rise to near unity. This establishes that there always exists a common profit rate, π^*, and that it is unique. Any other P will raise one π and lower the other.

We have arrived at the following fundamental result: there exists an unique set of prices, and of methods of production, which gives a rate of profit (*a*) common to all industries and (*b*) maximal in the sense that it is the highest that all can simultaneously attain. More specifically, if any other pair of techniques is chosen, either one industry has a lower profit rate if the other has an unchanged rate, or both have lower rates. Or again, if one secures a higher profit rate (with different prices and a new maximum profit technique), the other one must have a lower rate. This determination of prices and methods of production is 'best' only for profits and in itself implies nothing for the community. In fig. 2.2 by extending the two unit isoquants in equal proportion (keeping slopes unchanged) until the two extended isoquants have a common tangent running through the origin, the optimal method is the one leading to the tangent point and the common proportionate extension is the profit rate. The value of industry one's unit output is the projection of e_1 on p^*, perpendicular to the common tangent. The materials cost per unit is the projection of the best technique, a_1^*, and the profit per unit is the value less cost, i.e. the projection of net output per unit of gross output, u_1^*. The profit rate, π^*, is the ratio of profit to cost and is equal to the proportionate extension of a_1^*, $\pi^* a_1^*$. The line from a_1^* vertically to p^* also cuts e_1 in the same proportions. Since a_2^* has been extended in the same proportion, all the same conditions apply there. By a little experimentation it is easy to discover that no other set of prices and processes will give as high a common profit rate. The secret of the fundamental role of prices lies in the fact that the scalar product of prices and the various input vectors reduces complex, and hence incomparable, quantities to simple scalar costs, which are then easily compared as to magnitude.

That there always exists a unique positive profit rate is only true if the economy can exist, i.e. is viable or productive. In this simple model profit is synonymous with net product. It is significant that we cannot say from the inspection of any one set of techniques whether or not it can form a viable economy with others. Only from a simultaneous inspection of the two can we say whether they can exist as a self-sufficient economy with positive net product. Thus if the unit isoquant of 2 in fig. 2.1 were as shown and that of 1 were to lie below the line oh, there would be no price vector which yielded a positive profit with any pair of techniques in the two industries. Therefore no such economy could exist for any length of time. There will, for any p, always be one negative or both negative profit rates. The projections of the two profit rates on p give the net value added of each and their sum gives net national product and it will always be negative.

These same considerations define the limits within which p must lie in fig. 2.1. It cannot be further in the clockwise direction than P_u, perpendicular to ok, since here the greatest profit rate for 2 is zero and beyond this all techniques would yield negative profit rates. Similarly, there is a p_v which gives zero as the maximum profit rate for good 1 and any p further anti-clockwise than this would mean no production of good 1. Therefore p must lie

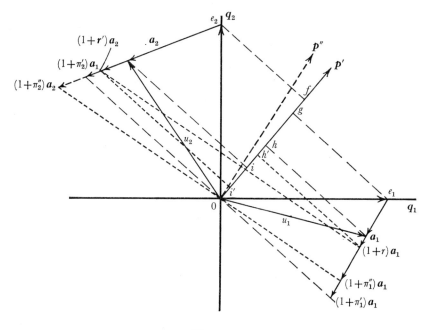

Fig. 2.3

between p_u and p_v; the narrower the angle between p_u and p_v the smaller is net output as a fraction of gross output and, other things being equal, the poorer the community. When the angle shrinks to zero, p_u and p_v coincident, the limit of viability has been reached; the community can produce enough to keep producing the required inputs but no more. In the next chapter it will become clearer that it is the maximizing of net as a fraction of gross output that is required to justify a common maximum profit rate and the choice of processes it dictates.

It is worthwhile to follow somewhat more closely the successive steps in a trial-and-error or iterative solution. Suppose that, on the basis of some historically determined prices, p', the producers have chosen their least cost, maximum profit techniques, a_1 and a_2, and that they do not, or cannot, alter these with subsequent price changes. In fig. 2.3 the value of unit output of good one is og, the cost of materials, prime cost, is hg and operating profit is oh. For sector two the same quantities are of, if and oi. Sector one can expect a profit rate, before interest, of oh/hg = π'_1, which, in this

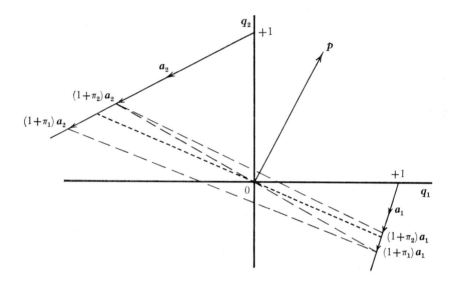

Fig. 2.4

case, is greater than π'_2 = oi/if. Assuming no risk, the capital market will supply funds at the same rate of interest, r', to both, the rate lying somewhere between π'_1 and π'_2. There are now costs of gh' for one and fj' for two, which give rise to some new pure profit rates. These pure profit rates represent disequilibrium to be corrected by raising p_2 and lowering p_1 until both pure profits are eliminated, leaving $\pi_1 = \pi_2 = r$. For the second round producers look at the only costs they know, the first round ones, and on this basis they announce their prices for the second round on the basis of the old prices marked up by r'. These prices, p'', depending on what r' is chosen may or may not have the same level as p', but since the price level makes no difference here, p'' can be taken to lie on the unit circle. To locate p'', draw a line from $(1+r')\,a_1$ to $(1+r')\,a_2$ and erect a perpendicular to it through the origin. To find, after the alterations in cost, the new, and unequal, profit rates, draw a line perpendicular to p'' through the origin, connecting the extensions of a_1 and of a_2. The profits and profit rate of two have gone up and those of one down. The rates, having come closer, there is now less freedom in the choice of r''.

Fig. 2.4 shows why this iterative process will in fact always discover the one and only set of prices which yields equal profit rates. Given a price vector and its normal through the origin, there results a pair of, usually different, profit rates in the two sectors. Take the profit rate on a_1 and draw a line to the point on the a_2 ray with a'_1s profit rate, and do the same for a_2 on a_1. The new interest rate must be chosen between the limits of the intersections of these lines with the cost vectors as is shown by the dotted line. The end-points of the new line lie within the range defined by the end points of the previous line through the origin. Yet the end points of the new line determine another pair of new lines that define the limits within which a further new pair of lines must be drawn. Therefore each step narrows the range within which r must be set, so that it converges ultimately to a single line yielding the same profits for both sectors, and this determines the price ray normal to it, which is the solution sought.

If the maximum profit technique is re-chosen each round, the problem is essentially the same and the solution is found in a similar way. The result is a common profit rate but now the greatest possible common profit rate.

2.6. Cross-field dynamics

Thus far we have been concerned with strictly dual dynamics, i.e. disequilibrium between price and cost led to alterations in prices until equilibrium was reached, and similarly disequilibrium in demand and supply led to alterations, in output. Walras held, however, that a divergence between supply and demand led to changes in price and Marshall studied the effects on output of differences between price and cost. What happens if we have both types of effects operative?

Of great importance is the speed of reaction. If prices are flexible, we may expect them to react rather quickly to imbalances in demand and supply (short run) but the reaction to profits is slow (long run). Slowest of all is any change in the technique of production; certainly short-run fluctuations in prices will not lead to changes in methods. Therefore the technique is taken as unchanged during the dynamic process, and then only considered as a kind of extra-long-run adaptation. Also, purely for simplification, consider only relative prices and outputs.

There is a given and unchanging final demand for net output. Further there is either a state bank or a capital market which sets a rate of interest somewhere between the highest and lowest operating profits, thus resulting in some positive and some negative net profits except in final equilibrium with all operating profits equal and equal to the rate of interest. With a given technique, there is always a unique equilibrium output $\bar{q}$, which equates supply and demand, and a unique $\bar{p}$ which equates operating profit rates or makes all profits zero with the interest rate equal to the operating profit rates.

Initially we do not know $\bar{p}$ or $\bar{q}$ and choose any arbitrary positive sets. All p can be divided into two classes, those counter clockwise (left) from $\bar{p}$ and those clockwise (right) from $\bar{p}$ and similarly for q and $\bar{q}$. There are then qualitatively four kinds of situation. For p left of $\bar{p}$, q to the left of $\bar{q}$ and q to the right of $\bar{q}$. For p to the right of $\bar{p}$, the same two cases, giving four cases in all.

If p is to the left, this favours good 2 by producing a positive profit (negative for good 1) so that q moves leftwards (i.e. good 2 is increasing and 1 decreasing). If q is to the left of $\bar{q}$ it moves away from equilibrium, but the supply for two being greater than demand, p moves right as shown in fig. 2.5 a. Therefore the price and profit rate of 2 both fall at an accelerating rate as q moves away from its equilibrium. There p reaches its equilibrium value but will be falling at its greatest rate (q at that point ceases moving leftwards and hence is at its maximum deviation from $\bar{q}$) and hence cannot come to rest there but must overshoot to the region to the right of $\bar{p}$, thus bringing us to a second class of situations illustrated in fig. 2.5 b. Now prices have become favourable to 1 and its profit rate is positive and 2 is experiencing a loss. Therefore output of 1 will be expanded and of 2 contracted, entailing motion of q rightwards. Output of 1 is still deficient, however, so prices will continue to move in favour of 1, i.e. p still moves rightwards as in b. Thus q will be propelled towards equilibrium at an accelerating pace, but cannot be arrested there and must fall through it, leading to the third class of situations, illustrated in fig. 2.6c. Now the production of 1 is excessive and of 2 deficient, so prices begin altering in favour of 2 and against 1 (p moves leftward). Though less 2 is produced than is demanded,

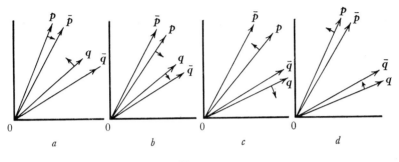

Fig. 2.5

it is still being produced at a loss, though at a diminishing loss, so q continues to move rightwards. Consequently p moves at an increasing rate to its equilibrium value but will pass through it, thus bringing us to the forth and last of the qualitative behaviour classes, shown in fig. 2.6d. p will continue leftwards but the fact that now 2 is profitable and 1 making losses, means that q has reversed direction and is now moving leftwards and towards its equilibrium, which it will reach and pass through. We will then be back in case a and have completed our survey of all the possible types and incidentally shown that this type of dynamical behaviour necessarily leads to interdependent cycles in prices, profits, outputs and inventories. It cannot approach and stay at equilibrium from one side only; it must overshoot and hence oscillate. What of stability? Will the savings get larger or smaller? This depends on the particular numbers involved and cannot be settled by the qualitative delineation of types, but what can be said is that if the speed of reaction (especially in output) is slow enough, the system can be stable. Then we shall gradually shrink on to the double equilibrium situations with $p = \bar{p}$ and $q = \bar{q}$, the rate of interest, lying always between π_1 and π_2, will come to equal both as they approach equality at equilibrium, leaving zero net profit for both industries.

Beginning without knowing the equilibrium prices and outputs, an economic system, following these rules of choice and assuming stability, will arive at the correct values after some, possibly considerable, time. However, we began with an arbitrary choice of technique which will not be optimal at our final equilibrium values. Once prices have settled down to their long-run values, managers should seek to discover any other known techniques which will yield them a positive net profit. They will then choose

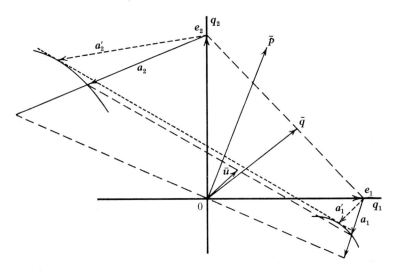

Fig. 2.6

the maximum profit techniques, a_1' and a_2', given the existing prices as shown in fig. 2.6 by the tangent line. But now the prices and outputs will no longer be the equilibrium ones with the new techniques. So that now there is one of the four types given above and the evolution will proceed as before until the new set of equilibrium outputs and prices will be found. Yet when these are established our techniques will no longer be optimal and further a technique can be chosen which will yield net positive profits for both industries. And then the whole process can be again repeated. Will these successive steps converge to the ultra long-run best techniques and corresponding set of prices at which it is no longer possible to find *any* techniques which will yield a positive profit for both, i.e. both net profit rates are at the social optimum, equal and zero? In section 2.4 we saw that if whenever the operating profit in one industry is higher than the other, its prices were to be lowered relative to the other, the system would tend toward the greatest common profit rate and its corresponding techniques. Here we have the same procedure (but in a more complicated form). Thus if $\pi_2 > \pi_1$, this will alter outputs in favour of 2 and this will mean a fall in p_2 relative to p_1, hence the effect is qualitatively the same though at one remove. Therefore it will ultimately arrive at the best techniques and equilibrium outputs and prices. Note that the *best* techniques and its corresponding $\bar{p}$ is independent of $\bar{q}$ and would not change were any change to be made in demand and hence $\bar{q}$.

3

THE DETERMINATION OF
RELATIVE OUTPUTS; DUALITY

3.1. Duality

Economics requires much minding of one's p's and q's, prices and quantities. We are thus committed to a dualism from the start, but what is not usually made clear is the nature of these twins; are they an identical pair, equal or symmetric or parallel, or are they quite different, unrelated, uncomparable. By the assumption of constant costs, the connection between the twins is severed and the duality of the economy is brought into sharp relief, which is helpful in revealing more about its nature.

As with prices, we seek not the absolute levels of outputs, but, initially, only relative outputs—how is productive activity allocated, at whatever level, amongst the various industries. Similarly, in answering this question we must also select the techniques appropriate to their allocation and these two questions can only be answered jointly. As with price and value, the analysis of output and production can be solved completely without any mention of the dual quantities. Yet great illumination and much simplification comes precisely from juxtaposing or combining the two.

3.2. Graphical representation of gross and net relative outputs

Gross outputs are total outputs and net outputs are the gross outputs less the quantities used up in producing those outputs. Until recently economists chose to ignore this structure of production and concentrated on net output, but with the increasing complexity of production, this becomes unsatisfactory. It is like discussing the performance of a runner in terms of his feet and ankles and ignoring legs and torso.

For simplicity assume each industry has chosen a single technique with inputs per unit of output, a_1 and a_2 and net outputs per unit of gross output u_1 and u_2, as in fig. 3.1. We wish to know what

24

will be the net output for any gross output or, conversely, what gross output will be required to produce any particular net output. This is most conveniently done by separating (thanks to constant costs) scale and proportion, or absolute and relative outputs.

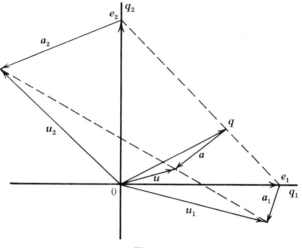

Fig. 3.1

The scale at which we operate each production process can be measured in terms of output. We separate scale from proportion by taking relative outputs as weights, i.e.

$$q_1 = \frac{Q_1}{Q_1 + Q_2} \quad \text{and} \quad q_2 = \frac{Q_2}{Q_1 + Q_2},$$

the Q's are absolute gross outputs and the q's are relative gross outputs, which, since they add to unity, can be treated as weights and applied to the net output vectors u_1 and u_2. Since q has unit sum, it will lie along a straight line between e_1 and e_2. If we produce only Q_1 we get a net output given by u_1 and if only Q_2, we get u_2. As q runs from e_1 to e_2, it goes through all positive ratios of the two goods. and we get net outputs, u, which run from u_1 and u_2, along the straight line connecting them (see section 1.6). q divides the line from e_1 to e_2 in this same proportion as u does the line u_1 to u_2. This serves to locate either one, given the other. q must in any case be restricted to the positive quadrant (negative gross output having no meaning) and it is usual, but not necessary

25

to be concerned with positive u as well, thus further restricting q to same range in between e_1 and e_2. q_1 and q_2 can be considered as weights applied to unit gross outputs e_1 and e_2; they give q lying on a straight line connecting them. Similarly, applied to u_1 and u_2, they give the locus of net output, u, stretching on a

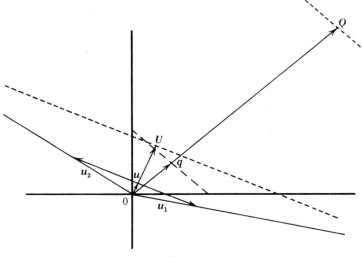

Fig. 3.2

straight line between them. Net output can also be found by subtracting the input vector, a, from the gross output vector, q. a can be found by applying the same weights q_1 and q_2 to a_1 and a_2, the input vectors; it also lies along a straight line connecting their end points, but its base must be taken as the tip of q. The a vector, for any given q, may then be visualized in fig. 3.1 as swinging along the locus of q from slope a_1 to slope a_2.

This then gives the relative allocation of productive effort required for any relative demand for net output, quite independently of scale. To take account of scale, given a desired net output U, as in fig. 3.2, find that u lying along the same ray and determines what multiple the length of U is of u. Then find the corresponding q, multiply it by the same multiple, thus obtain the scale and projections of the required gross output Q. This covers all net outputs lying between the rays to infinity, upon which u_1 and u_2 lie, and all positive gross outputs.

3.3. Optimal output with many techniques

Now consider many techniques available to each industry. By contrast with value theory, there is no question of an optimal decision for each industry since they are not trying to maximize output and there is no meaning to minimizing a collection of inputs. Therefore we must turn to the collectivity to define a social optimum for all industries taken as an interdependent whole. But even then the problem is somewhat complicated by the fact that there are no upper limits to outputs. Consequently we cannot define an optimum as one in which it is impossible to increase one output keeping the other constant, for it is always possible to increase both outputs.

In section 2.5 we saw what techniques and what prices would be chosen by profit maximizing producers free to shift between industries. There is, however, no indication of whether the result is optimal—for this we must look at the outputs available from this choice. In section 3.1 we saw what outputs are available but we cannot compare these possibilities unless we value them with the help of the prices established in the dual. Thus it is only by conjoining the twin systems that we can assess the optimality of a profit maximizing procedure.

In fig. 3.3 the profit maximal price set is p^* and we can value outputs by taking its dot product with outputs. If we produce only good 1, its value is $e_1 \cdot p^* = c_1 + u_1$, cost plus net product or surplus; cost is $a_1 \cdot p^* = c_1$ and surplus is $u_1 \cdot p^* = u_1$. Similarly if we produce only good 2, we get a different value $e_2 \cdot p^* = c_2 + u_2$ with $u_2 \cdot p^* = u_2$. But then the net product is the same fraction of gross product in both industries. Since the proportion of net to gross value product is the same in both industries, it will be the same for allocation of production in any proportion between the two. Therefore as we let q run from e_1 to e_2 and u from u_1 to u_2, the total product value of net as a proportion of gross value product is a constant $= u_1/(c_1 + u_1) = u_2/(c_2 + u_2)$. Since the line giving the projection of u on p^* is tangent to the unit isoquant, it follows, as will be seen by inspection of fig. 3.3, that any other technique chosen, in either industry, will yield a net value product which is a smaller percentage of gross value product. Hence for any given gross output whatsoever, the largest net value product will emerge from the profit maximizing choice of techniques; it is, in this sense, the socially optimal set of production processes.

In somewhat unprecise form this notion has been the central theme of economics from Adam Smith onwards in the form of the 'unseen hand' and *laissez-faire*. However, only with Walras and more particularly Pareto was the proposition properly formulated and thence all the recent formulations.

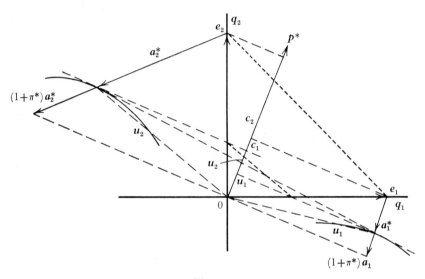

Fig. 3.3

It could be called the fundamental theorem of the economic calcalus. Its remarkable conclusion is that a social maximum under the correct conditions, can come about although no one tries to achieve it.† This gives meaning and sense to what is in itself without sense or meaning—the free trading in a market place. It explains how an essentially unsolvable practical problem of production is in fact solved all the time and why this solution makes some sense. It has often been used to justify private property and capitalism but in fact is politically neutral, being just as, or perhaps more applicable to a socialist or communist economy.

† Each producer is maximizing profit but no one is maximizing the aggregate net value product.

3.4. The Samuelson substitution theorem

One result of especial importance is the consequence, first perceived by Professor Samuelson, that with constant costs, the choice of best technique is independent of demand. If we choose the best technique for any one output, since costs are constant, it will be best also for any other output whatsoever. This result is so powerful because it allows us to separate the economic problem into demand and outputs and solve each independently of the other. Thus in fig. 3.3, we can get our result without even specifying either q or u. Therefore if we have the best set of possible results for unit sum level and any allocation, then we have it for any output whatsoever. Consequently, for optimal ('efficient') production, we get an asymmetry between p and q, for the latter can be anything positive (strictly, non-negative) whereas the former must have one particular value p^*. So long, then, as our assumptions hold, we need not consider the unit isoquants or some list of known alternate techniques, but can restrict ourselves to a single a and u for each industry. How great a simplification this is can only be seen in practice, as will appear subsequently. In particular it is the theoretical justification of input–output analysis which is central to a great range of applied planning and forecasting analyses.

3.5. The temporal element in production and the von Neumann ray

Let us now introduce in the simplest possible way, the basic unavoidable dynamic aspect of production, ie. that inputs must *precede* outputs (an aspect thus far ignored). All processes take the same, unit, length of time. Production during any period t accrues as output, q in the next period, $t+1$. Thus last period's production accrues in this period as output to add to stockpiles and this period's inputs, governed by next period's outputs subtract from stockpiles. Further, we continue to ignore the problem of wages, either workers live on air or else a conventional wage is paid in kind and is included in our unit input vector, a. It takes a inputs to produce one unit of a good; to produce 1·10 units will require 1.10 a and so for any proportionate variation, e.g. 0·85 a or 1·25 a, we need only extend or shorten the length of a appropriately.

Since outputs this year depend on inputs from last year's output, the scale of output is indeterminate. Restricting the problem to a common scale variation of the two industries, if outputs this year are made lower than last year, consumption can be larger this year than last year without running down stocks. Such disinvestment impoverishes the economy so that next year both output and

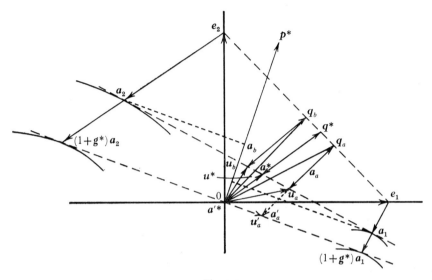

Fig. 3.4

consumption must be lowered even to maintain the lower level of output. On the other hand if output is increased this year over last year, inputs must be increased (investment) so consumption must be decreased if stocks are not to be run down.

Now consider an economy dedicated to maximum expansion of the scale of output. All profit or surplus is used for the expansion of output and this is done by simply expanding the scale of output each period by enough to absorb the whole of last period's outputs as inputs. In fig. 3.4 the line e_1 to e_2 gives the locus of gross output (relative), e.g. q_a and q_b. These give rise to the locus of net outputs e.g. u_a and u_b, which are gross outputs less inputs, thus determining the locus of inputs, e.g. a_a and a_b. As q runs from e_1 to e_2, a runs from a_1 to a_2 with its base at q and tip at u. For a predominance of q_2 output u lies to the left of q as at q_b, and for a predominance of q_1, to the right as at q_a. Somewhere in between will lie the point at which u coincides with the direction of q, i.e. at q^* and u^*. This is clearly the state of the economy which we seek, for steady, balanced growth at an equal rate in all sectors. We seek an input vector a equal and opposite to the gross output vector q, so that u is reduced to zero, i.e. along q^*. If we increase both rates of output in the proportion g^*, this will likewise increase all input vectors in this proportion to a' the locus of which will lie along the line connecting $(1 + g^*)$ a_1 and $(1 + g^*)a_2$ and passing through the origin. If we produce in the proportion of q_a, we get inputs of a'_a and net product of u'_a, i.e. additions to stocks of good 1 and drawing down of stocks of good 2. But if we alter the proportion of gross outputs to q^*, a'^* is at the origin and we exactly use up all last period's output as this period's inputs. If we were to keep output constant at $q = q^*$, we would have $u = u^*$ and $a = a^*$, so that inputs and net outputs are both proportional to gross outputs q^*. This surplus being in the same proportion as inputs could be devoted to accumulation, i.e. to providing the inputs for a proportional expansion of outputs. Since expanding both sectors in the proportion of g^* just exhausts these surpluses, we know that $u^* = g^* a^*$ and hence also that $q^* = u^* + a^* = (1 + g^*)a^*$.

Given a pair of techniques, e.g. a_1 and a_2 in fig. 3.4, the vector of prices, p^*, which gives an equal profit rate is perpendicular to the locus of the expanded inputs a'. For sector one the value of the product is the projection on p^* of e_1, the cost is the projection of a_1 and the profit rate is the ratio of the projection of g^*a_1 to that of a_1, which is simply g^*, so that $\pi = g^*$ for both sectors. Therefore the greatest possible growth rate is equal to the common profit rate for the two sectors. Therefore there exists for any pair of processes a common profit rate equal to their greatest common growth rate, g^*, called the eigenvalue of the system. It is associated with a unique proportion of outputs, q^*, called the eigenvector (or eigenray since it holds for any scale) of outputs, and with a unique price vector, the eigenvector of prices (or eigenray since only relative prices are determined). Though the two eigenvalues are equal, the two eigenrays of the system are not the same. Thus any viable economy has two eigenrays and a single eigenvalue associated with it.

Each pair of processes will have an eigenvalue; amongst all the viable pairs of processes constituting a known technology, there will be one or more with the greatest eigenvalues. This greatest amongst all the greatest growth rates, may be called the von Neumann eigenvalue after its discoverer. For a convex technology, as in fig. 3.4 there will always be one and only one pair of processes which have the von Neumann eigenvalue. To discover it, extend progressively the unit isoquants until their common tangent passes through the origin. This gives the locus of all possible inputs for the expanded scale of outputs, $(1 + g^*)a$, and the input which leads from q back to the origin, is the required solution, since all last year's outputs are exactly used up by this year's inputs. This g^* is the greatest of all the maximum growth rates, since for any other pair of techniques, the locus of inputs passes below the origin and hence for no output could inputs be covered out of last year's output. Stated another way, keeping one sector's growth rate at g^* with its associated process, any alteration of process in the other sector would require a lowering of its growth rate if input is not to exceed available output. Or, again, keeping input and output equal, the growth rate of one sector could only be increased by reducing that of the other.

Here there is a much more straightforward social optimum. If the society has as its goal maximum growth rate, then there is a clear and unique result: the von Neumann eigenvalue tells us what that greatest growth rate is, the associated price eigenray tells us how to value the outputs, and the quantity eigenray tells us how to allocate the total productive effort between the various sectors. Only relative prices and relative outputs are determined, but here one must note a striking lack of symmetry between the dual concepts. Whether p is rising, falling or constant is not fundamentally important. By contrast, it is basic to know whether and by how much the scale of q is increasing; in fact this is precisely what gives the eigenvalue its significance. In the case of prices the eigenvalue gives the profit rate and leaves the dynamics of prices indeterminate. Where, as here, we are seeking the greatest common growth rate, it is a simple matter to identify the social optimum—the various choices are each represented by a single number, the eigenvalue, and the greatest one is best. It is for this reason that it is possible to find the optimum in terms of outputs only, without valuing them. In all other cases it is impossible to compare different baskets of goods without first valuing the goods so that they can be added to a single comparable number.

By comparison of fig. 3.4 and 2.4 it becomes clear that the operation of a profit rate and a growth rate is exactly the same; they both require equal proportional extension of the input vectors a. Therefore if we have selected the $p = p^*$ which gives the greatest profit rate π^*, then this same technique will give the greatest growth rate $g^* = \pi^*$, because both do the same thing, extending the two input vectors a until the line connecting them passes through the origin. In fig. 3.4 the lower pair of isoquants represents the locus of the input vectors of all input techniques undergoing expansion at rate g^*. It is immediately evident that a line connecting any two other techniques would pass below the origin and hence require more inputs than there are outputs available. Similarly for prices. Any other pair of techniques, having an interest cost equal to π^* would experience losses in both sectors. Another important asymmetry appears between p and q: we do not care whether p is rising, falling or constant; relative p is all that matters. Whereas, not only relative but even more absolute q matters and, what is more, the two are intimately linked through growth rate which determines uniquely the relative outputs. It is also important to note that, if our sole aim is growth, we can define a choice of best techniques, i.e. one which will produce the maximum common growth rate, quite independently of prices and value. For all other cases goods must be valued in order to make them comparable, but requiring equal growth rates allows us to compare different output sets without valuation.

3.6. Optimal consumption and optimal growth; simplest accumulation problem

So long as the temporal structure of production is ignored, the scale of output is arbitrary—the greater the output, the greater the input available and the greater the surplus. So there can be no question of a maximum output or consumption; the only thing that can be maximised is the proportional growth rate, which applies to any scale of output. But the moment account is taken of the fact that inputs must precede output, the position is quite altered. In the short run the scale of production is completely determined by the available outputs from last period. Consumption plus inputs now must equal outputs from last period, except that either may exceed the other for short periods and in modest amounts through growth or decline of stocks. Consideration of an active role of stocks is reserved for section 6.5, but here stocks are taken to be essentially passive and enabling. Last period's output sets the scale of current production (taken as unit sum magnitude). The maximum maintainable consumption is immediately found by drawing the straight line tangent to both unit isoquants as

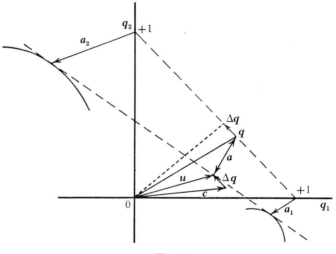

Fig. 3.5

shown in fig. 3.5. The consumption $c = u$ can be produced indefinitely by choosing the optimal pair of techniques a_1 and a_2, which yield more of both goods than any other known pair of techniques. The composition of gross and net outputs are arbitrarily given by last period's outputs, but these may be altered to any desired proportion in a series of steps in which $c + \Delta q = u$, as indicated in fig. 3.5. Therefore the Samuelson Substitution Theorem holds for relative outputs. Some variation of stocks results but they are thereafter ignored and have no significant role. A comparison with fig. 3.4 will show that the optimal choice of techniques for growth is necessarily different from that for consumption, since the tangents determining the techniques are different in the two cases. For growth there is the unique von

Neumann eigenray, given by q^*, whereas here relative gross outputs may be whatever desired consumption dictates. More important still is the fact that competitive profit maximizers will choose the optimal techniques for growth but, in consequence, will always be producing a sub-optimal output of consumption goods.

Just as with relative outputs, the scale of output can be altered to any extent, given time. The problem consists of the gradual accumulation of any desired scale of inputs and of consumption. By consuming less now, more may consumed later, which is precisely the traditional accumulation problem. Thus suppose an economy has considerable unemployment but a constant population. It wishes to expand consumption to some higher level, c, with its required q. The simplest procedure would be to reduce consumption below net output, and, keeping it below, allow gross and net output to grow in their existing proportions until the target scale values are reached. The question is: would this be optimal, and the answer is, no.

There are two aspects to the problem—the pace of growth, and the structure of relative outputs along with the associated question of appropriate techniques. A proper discussion of the first is postponed to section 7.1, and in its place the following program is outlined: in an initial period consumption is reduced below net output, so that an increment to stocks accrues; in the following period consumption is restored to its previous level and, with output is left unaltered throughout; because of constant costs, the increment to stocks may be treated quite separately from the continuing constant consumption and production; if it is desired to grow as rapidly as possible with this single act of saved-up resources, the increments must lie on the von Neumann eigenray and the techniques to be used with them must be the optimal growth ones; neither output proportions nor techniques will be the same as those of the continuing constant level output; therefore as rapidest growth proceeds, the over-all output vector will veer increasingly towards the von Neumann eigenray of outputs; however, as the process approaches the target level, the output vector must veer back to its original proportions in order to allow consumption to rise and ultimately absorb the whole of net output; likewise techniques must gradually be shifted back to the original ones for consumption optimality; in fact, section 7.1 suggests that, for intertemporal optimality, consumption must be increased throughout the process until, in the end, it equals net output and brings the process to a close; this program is a primitive example of what is known as the Turnpike Theorem; in abstract economic spaces, the shortest distance between two points is not the quickest.

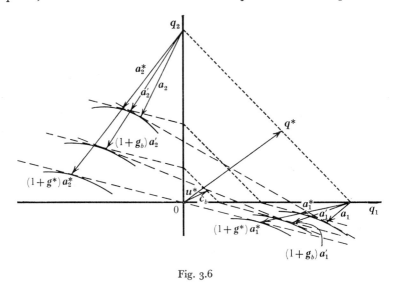

Fig. 3.6

All this can be illustrated in a single diagram where successive scales of output are reduced to an arbitrary unit sum scale, as in fig. 3.6. Initially there is an optimal output with the best techniques a_1 and a_2, with all surplus consumed in any desired proportion, e.g. q_0 and c_0. Then there is a single act of saving which then becomes the von Neumann eigenvector q^*, with units redefined to unit sum scale. Suppose that in the first period, maximum growth is undertaken. The techniques (incremental) a_1^* and a_2^* must be chosen and the scale of output set at $1+g^*$ such that the inputs a^* just absorb the whole of the increments to stocks. The maximum consumption possible with this growth rate is zero; any other techniques would yield negative consumption, i.e. would require a reduction of stocks. Thereafter in successive periods, consumption is gradually raised resulting in a decelerating growth rate until terminal consumption absorbs the whole of the incremental net output, i.e. the entire increase of net output over its initial level. To find what is the best result for any

36

state of the process as g falls from g^* to zero, expand the isoquants in some common proportion, e.g. g_b in fig. 3.6, and connect these expanded isoquants by their common tangent. This chooses the best techniques, which will lie between a_1 and a_1^* and between a_2 and a_2^*, since the slope of this tangent gradually alters as g falls from g^* to zero. The result is the set of greatest possible consumptions for any given growth rate, g_b. Any consumption along this line is available, e.g. c_b, which may be different in proportions from c_0 because of the higher standard of consumption. Thus we see that optimal consumption divides into two pure cases—zero growth rate and maximal growth rate, and that all other cases are a blend of the two. In this fashion it is possible to analyze whatever successive values of c and of g may be found to be optimal for the pace of accumulation between initial and final states of the economy.

3.7. Aggregate income equals net value product; Say's Law

The sum of all incomes earned (or net value added) will always equal the sum of the value of all net products, identically, that is, no matter what prices are and outputs are. The reason that they are identically equal for any p and q is that these two quantities, income and net product, are sums of the same things merely added in a different order. In fig. 3.7 we have to show that the vertical projection (value of net output) of u on p is equal to the sum of the projections of u_1 and u_2 on p each weighted by the relative outputs, this latter being net incomes per unit output weighted by the number of units. The value of incomes earned is the weighted sum of the projections of u_1 and u_2 on p. The value of net output is the projection of u on p, but u is the weighted sum of u_1 and u_2, so that the projection of the weighted sum of the u's must equal the weighted sum of the projections of the u's. This can be seen to be so by decomposing u into the weighted sum of the u's and seeing that their projections identically add to that of u.

The precise content of Say's Law has never been satisfactorily agreed on by economists, Say himself having written somewhat ambiguously, but its broad import is plain. Aggregate supply equals aggregate demand even though it need not be so for each good. This result follows from the equality of aggregate value of incomes and outputs subject to two vital further assumptions. If all incomes are spent for goods and if their spending coincides in time with the sale of the net product which gave rise to them. This venerable 'Law' is no law since not only is it not invariably true, it is never true because both assumptions are false. However, economists cannot be too choosy about the company they keep (having no proper laws at all) and the fact is that Say's Law is

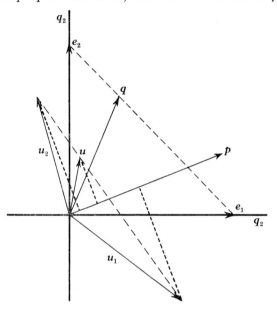

Fig. 3.7

substantially true most of the time and provides a most useful insight, an insight vouchsafed only after some acquaintance with economic analysis. Thus a shoe manufacturer raising his output of shoes will not experience an increase in his demand whereas, as every economist knows, a nation increasing its general level of output will tend to have a similar increase in demand. It is a most compliant law stating that an economy will happily rest at any level it is moved to. The economy can therefore be said to be roughly in neutral equilibrium at any scale. One particular aspect of Says's Law is conveniently exhibited in fig. 3.8. For any p and q, the value of gross output is $q \cdot p = og$, the cost of inputs, $a \cdot p = hg$, and the value of income earned is $q \cdot p - a \cdot p = u \cdot p = oh$. Incomes earned, if they are all spent on net output will necessarily equal the value of that net output, i.e. $u.p$. Given some output q, a is uniquely determined, and so is the total value of income, but not what it may be spent on. It is convenient to reverse the direction of the demand vector for net output, u, so that it may be added to a to give demand for gross output. Subject

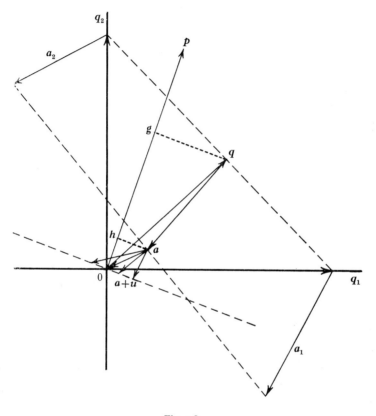

Fig. 3.8

to the condition of spending all earned income, the locus of possible demands for gross output is a line through the origin perpendicular to p ($a+u$ in fig. 3.8). Complete equilibrium requires $a+u$ to be equal and opposite to q, i.e. to rest on the origin. But it may equally well be in the north–west or south–east quadrants and it will still be satisfying Say's Law. Excess demand for one good implies deficient demand for the other, i.e. aggregate supply and demand are equal, but partial supply and demand need not be. If income receivers spend more than their incomes the locus of $a + u$ will lie below the origin and if they spend less, it will lie above. In both these cases, Say's Law is invalid; there is general disequilibrium as well.

3.8. Decentralized planning

The analysis of the nature of a planned economy brings great insight to the study of a free market mechanism; conversely, the functioning of a pricing system is fundamental to the understanding of the problems of planning. There is growing interest amongst planners in the related question of to what extent and in what ways they can use some sort of price-market mechanism to improve on the performance of planned economies.

In this simple model there exists a unique, optimal combination of prices, outputs and techniques. Though it exists, actually to realize it is an altogether different and more difficult task. The complicated question of stability arises: will this optimal solution be attained under specified conditions, and, if realized but being displaced, will the optimal state be regained? A related question is: can we, by computer or otherwise, calculate the optimal solutions? One of the most hopeful lines of attack is to create a somewhat special market mechanism which will function as an analogue computer, thus, hopefully, rendering this huge problem more tractable. Such a mechanism will only achieve its object if it is stable, i.e. if it has a 'homing' tendency to close onto the correct solution.

Suppose all productive enterprises to be owned collectively and to be directed by hired managers who run them in the interest of the whole community much as they are now supposed to be doing for the private owners in capitalism. The state issues directives giving decision rules. Furthermore, suppose, for simplicity, that all consumption is rationed and that rations are issued and invariable used to a fixed amount. The objective is then to produce enough net outputs to satisfy the constant known consumption. What is not known is what gross outputs are necessary to achieve this.

The nature of the problem is easily seen from fig. 3.9. Reversing the direction of the total input vector A, add it to the known consumption $\hat{U}$ to get the unknown total gross output, Q. With a given technique in operation, Q will then be a complex multiple of $\hat{U}$, i.e. there will be a multiplier for each good separately. This result is independent of scale and hence applies to relative outputs, absolute outputs or to any increments to outputs. Thus if net output of good 1 is to be increased by od, then the output of good 1 must be increased by oe and the multiplier is oe/od, and

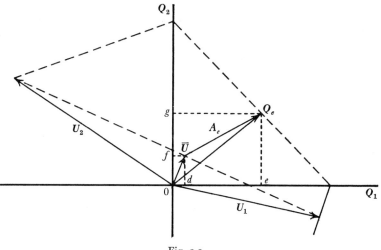

Fig. 3.9

similarly for the other sector. These multipliers (as many as there are goods) are in some ways analogous to the Kahn–Keynes aggregative multiplier, but they are at once more fundamental but also cruder. No propensity to save or to consume is involved, but rather only unavoidable technological relations. On the other hand the difference is somewhat more apparent than real because the most important components of saving come from the operating profits of productive enterprises, as here. The size of the multiplier for each sector depends on the whole structure of costs for all sectors. The overall effect on scale depends on the degree of viability; the nearer the angle between u_1 and u_2 to 180°, the greater will be the scale of gross output for a given net output.

The solution to the problem for two goods is simple enough, but the question is: can it be found for a system involving thousands of goods, and, in particular, can it be found by trial-and-error methods? The most remarkable and illuminating fact is that the system itself, if stable, can be made to compute the answer to its own problem. Each sector must have a given production process and sufficient stocks to fill in transitory gaps. Managers may be given the simplest possible decision rule: set this period's output at the level of last period's sales. Following this rule of quantity adjustment, the production of each good will gradually move into coincidence with the amount demanded.

To see why this is necessarily so, it is convenient to separate the problem of scale from that of proportions. Say's Law does not hold since there is no way of knowing the scale at which to produce, so that there may be excessive or deficient demand for all or most goods. The stability of the system arises from its viability, i.e. its ability to produce net output and hence its ability to exist at all. This means that inputs are less than outputs. Initially there is simply the given consumption demand; the second period's output is made equal to the initial demand; demand therefore in the second period consists of the consumption plus demand for inputs which is somewhat smaller; output in the third period then goes up again but by a smaller amount and so forth. Since the added inputs are always smaller than the added outputs, the increments to the scale of output, whether positive or negative, must have a diminishing magnitude. At an ever diminishing pace the economy gradually approaches a scale of output large enough to yield a net output large enough to cover the fixed consumption demand.

Though the scale of output may be correct, the individual outputs need not be. Suppose in fig. 3.9 that initially Q lies to the right of the final equilibrium Q_e; then A also lies to the right of A_e and of $\bar{U}$. The gradual addition of A to the fixed U will pull Q leftwards, towards equilibrium. If the on other hand we start with Q equal to $\bar{U}$, it lies to the left of equilibrium; the addition of the resulting A to $\bar{U}$ shifts Q rightwards and towards equilibrium. The decision rule always produces movement towards the equilibrium. Q may move in a series of diminishing steps towards equilibrium but it may also overshoot, depending on scale, cost structure and the initial situation. This raises the possibility of the system's proportions moving in ever widening swings from left to right. It can be shown, however, that this oscillatory instability is ruled out by viability, so that it will settle down to the correct proportions as well as the correct scale with supply and demand in balance in detail as well as in aggregate. Although it is helpful to separate scale and proportion they in reality always occur jointly. No producer can tell whether a deficient output is due to a scale imbalance or to one in his particular industry. This problem and its solution give the essence of input–output analysis (Ch. 7): to produce a given list of additional net outputs, by how much must gross outputs be increased? This can, in principle, be reckoned out in advance by computer and the move made to final equilibrium in one step. Or it can be, as here, reckoned out in the process of doing it, so that the solution is only gradually revealed as it comes into actual operation. This particular decision rule leads to a slow approach to the final equilibrium; more sophisticated rules can be used producing a more rapid convergence to the equality of supply and demand. Speed is important because it reduces the size of stocks it is necessary to carry during the transient adaptation. It is to be noted, however, that stability, and hence solubility, is not a property of the technical structure along but includes the decision rules as well. Thus if managers try to rebuild depleted stocks or to unload swollen stocks, the system very easily becomes unstable, and, far from equating supply and demand, developes ever greater excesses and deficiencies.

More difficult, both for centralized and for decentralized planning, is the problem of finding the best techniques as well as scale and proportions. In this case prices and money values are bound to be involved, so a process adapted from that of section 2.5 may be employed. There is a state bank which lends each period the entire capital required for all costs and receives back the loan at the end of the period plus interest at a common rate r. In addition the state receives all net profits and pays for all net losses. To simplify let us ignore the time lags and suppose the state receives and spends all interest (rentier) income as well as the difference between net profits and losses within the same production period. The consequences of this is that Say's Law holds: the aggregate value of both net and gross output equals the aggregate demand for it. The state either spends the money itself or gives social dividends on any principle to individuals or groups who spend all they receive. This demand for net product is in some given proportions, $\bar{u}$. The managers know the various available techniques.

In the beginning all is chaos; no one knows what prices should be and hence what techniques to use or what output to produce. The state initially makes a guess at prices and outputs and the rate of interest. It directs the managers to choose the most profitable technique (*vide* section 2.3) and to produce an intial output. The mangers thereafter control their own prices and outputs and are directed to act as follows: if they make a profit, reduce their price next period, if a loss, increase it, and if their output is greater than their demand, reduce output, if less than, increase it. If profits predominate over losses, the state bank is directed to raise

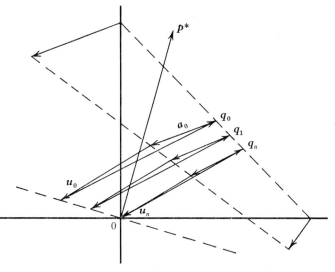

Fig. 3.10

the rate of interest, and if losses predominate, to lower it. The price and output developments are separated. Proceeding thus by trial and error, prices will gradually become optimal, von Neumann prices and the best techniques will be utilized, with only one technique used in each industry. The rate of interest will gradually be raised or lowered until it just absorbs all operating profits and net profits go to zero, there being in each industry only one technique which will just cover all costs including interest cost. All other techniques would result in losses. Some goods will be found to have no techniques which can cover costs and they cease production. Thus we determine not only which techniques will be used but also which goods will not be produced.

44

We could work out the evolution of prices and quantities simultaneously, but to simplify let us assume that the Neumann prices have been already found and are kept constant. From fig. 3.8 we know that gross demand will lie on a line perpendicular to p^* and passing through the origin. The demand for final product will always lie in the same direction but may vary in amount. In fig. 3.10 the demand for good 1 in excessive and for good 2 is deficient. Therefore the relative output of 1 is increased and that of 2 decreased, from say, q_0 to q_1, which reduces the partial disequilibrium. Proceeding thus we will tend towards q_{11} which will produce net output in the desired proportions and amounts. The scale of output remains what it was initially and is arbitrary.

3.9. The realization problem; sketch of disequilibrium dynamics

Say's Law is wrong in many ways, but its most profound, most fundamental, wrongness lies in the fact that expenditures connected with production do not coincide with finished output. Mostly these outlays come before, but in the case of profits, after. Last year's output is bought this year to carry on current production, which will be sold next year. A stationary economy presents no problem, but one undergoing change can present the most intractable difficulties.

First, consider a planned economy with a ministry of production which sets output targets and collects a turnover tax at a common flat rate on the value of output. The tax proceeds are disbursed as a social dividend which is entirely spent on consumption in a given proportion. There is a state bank which lends enterprizes the money for inputs in one year and is repaid next year out of receipts, with realized profits constituting a rate of return. With a given technique, taxes τ, consumption $\bar{c}$, there is a set of prices $\bar{p}$ which will yield an equal profit rate in the two sectors (fig. 3.11). For equilibrium $(1+\bar{g})\,\bar{a}$ plus $\bar{c}$ must add to last period's output $\bar{q}$ where the common growth rate equals the common profit rate. Such a single diagram can describe a continuous equilibrated growth by the device of reducing each quantity back to unit level each year. It is, however, most important to remember that $\bar{q}$ refers to last period's output and that current production only becomes available next period. Thus though aggregate demand for output equals the value of output, this has nothing to do with Say's Law, since it is expenditure from this period's production on last period's production, and the two productions are not equal. The solution $\bar{q}$ exists but need not be realized, if q lies nearer the origin or further from the origin, then the value of aggregate demand is not equal to the value of aggregate supply. This is the problem of scale, but there is also the problem of proportions, i. e. q to the right or to the left of $\bar{q}$.

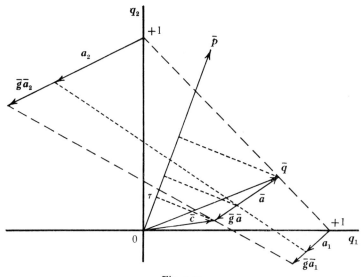

Fig. 3.11

Taking proportions as somehow correct, the question is how much enterprizes can realize on last period's investment. Suppose that last period the state bank took a view as to how much money it should lend and rationed loans to every enterprize that claimed they could achieve a rate of return r. A different group of bureaucrats in the ministry have this period set a common target of a growth rate of g. If g is less than r, the interest rate is unrealizable. Either prices are maintained with stocks of goods unsold so that, though book profits are there, the revenue is not sufficient to pay interest, or prices are reduced giving insufficient profits, both book and realized. A g greater than r means either a rundown of stocks or a price rise or both, with appropriate effects on profit rates.

46

The state bank receives back during the period, as repayment with interest, exactly what it lends out during the period for the purchase of inputs. Having lent last period $a \cdot p$ and lending this period $(1 + g) \ a \cdot p$, it receives a rate of return $r = g$, entirely determined by its own action as directed by the ministry. Thus they make their own results, except that they cannot push g above $\bar{g}$. If there is to be a constant price level, with supply equal to demand, r and g must equal $\bar{g}$. Hence the bank must increase the quantity of money lent (and hence the quantity of money) at the rate $\bar{g}$ each period, as is natural if output at constant prices increases at this rate. That the state by its own action determines the rate of return is an example of the Marxian realization problem. The same problem is endemic in capitalism where, in Kalecki's formulation, workers spend what they get and capitalists get what they spend.

Suppose in a free market economy with rigid prices, entrepreneurs set g below $\bar{g}$. Unsold output results in undesired additions to stocks. The entrepreneurs will then cut back their expansion rate to avoid further undesired growth in stocks, but, in the next period this only makes a bad situation worse. Or if they have set g too high, stocks are run down so that, in an effort to catch up, they step up g, leading to ever more violent decline in stocks. This is a primitive form of the 'knife edge' problem, which is a rediscovery, in post-Keynesian analyses, of the Marxian problem. Thus we see that Say's Law provides no comfort for the free market fundamentalist. The private enterpreneur can only invest if he knows, or thinks he knows, what other entrepreneurs will invest in the future. This leads to self-fulfilling prophecies of gloom or glory. The history of capitalism has fully exemplified this with alternations between buoyant demand, high profits, considerable inflation and depressed markets, unemployment, low profits.

In this situation central planning posesses a striking advantage over decentralized decision making. To the planner, unlike the plant manager, the appearance of unexpected stocks is not a disaster but rather a happy chance to increase the rate of expansion. Thus if he has put g too low, he will accelerate instead of decelerating, and if too high, he will then decelerate, moving, in both cases towards equality of demand and supply.

With a disequilibrium of proportions not of scale, the result is quite different. Private entrepreneurs will tend to decelerate where there is excess supply and accelerate where there is excess demand. In both cases this will tend to correct particular imbalances of supply and demand. This suggests the possibility that planners might be tempted into the disastrous course of increasing the growth rate of those sectors already producing too much and decreasing that of those under-producing. Seeing the whole rather than the part, they are unlikely to do so. The demand for good i comes from other sectors, unlike aggregate output where an increase in output means one in demand as well. A rise in the stocks of i should lead the planner to lower the growth rate of i and raise that of other sectors. Therefore with a mixture of growing and declining stocks, some growth rates will go up and others down, with the average roughly unchanged. Disequilibria in scale and proportion are usually mixed; thus if rising stocks predominate there will be a reshuffling of growth rates but with a higher average rate.

By varying growth rates it is clearly very difficult to find the right scale and proportions of output. Perhaps the best way to formulate the problem is in terms of cross-field dynamics as set forth in section 2. 6. In a system in which consumption is a constant proportion of aggregate output, there is an inherent profit and growth rate. The question is, for a planned economy, how to find it, and, for a market economy, whether, once removed, it will tend to evolve back to it.

By varying the price level, profits can be increased or decreased to any extent, but since costs vary in the same way, the profit rate is unaffected. By altering relative prices, some profit rates are raised whilst others are lowered, so that the average rate shows great stability. If growth rates in each sector are equal to profit rates, there will tend to be a stable aggregative growth rate. Taking $\bar{p}$ as the price vector that yields equal profit rates after taxes and $\bar{q}$ as the output vector which equates each individual supply to demand, fig. 2.5 may be used to analyze the dynamic behaviour of the system. In case (a) p and q are both to the left of their equilibrium values. Profit rate 2 is greater than that of 1, as are, then, their growth rates with the results that q rotates leftwards. q being to the left of its equilibrium value, the demand for 1 is greater than supply and the reverse for 2, so that the price of 1 raises relative to the price of 2, rotating p to the right. This process continues until p reaches its equilibrium value, which arrests the motion of q and fixes its maximum deviation from equilibrium. This means that p passes through $\bar{p}$ with maximum velocity and case (b) arises with p and q on opposite sides of their equilibrium values. Both now rotate rightwards since profit and growth rates of 1 are greater than those of 2 and there is excess demand for one and excess supply for 2. Hence q now comes into equilibrium, with p at its maximum deviation, and q rotating clockwise at its maximum rate. Thus to case (c) with both to the right of their equilibria. They now rotate in opposite directions with p returning to and passing through its equilibrium value. This returns the system to case (a) and completes and recommences a cycle.

Thus given the combined Marshall and Walras dynamic market behaviour, a cyclical variation in growth rates occurs. There is particular disequilibrium, unequal growth rates, but an overall long run constant growth rate is achieved. There is no assumption that Say's Law holds. The important question of whether, in the absence of continuing disturbances, these cycles will die out, is not easily answered. An intuitive argument may be made as follows: the economy is viable; viable economies are stable in prices and in outputs separately; a dynamic chain that goes from quantities to prices and back to quantities, is stable at each step and hence is stable over the whole process.

4

DISTRIBUTION AND PRODUCTION; LABOUR A FACTOR

4.1. Reformulation of the model in per capita terms

No actual economy does function without labour cost, even though it may be desirable in some cases. Therefore it is necessary to include labour explicitly, but to do so in two dimensions means stating everything per head. Strictly it must be per man-hour or man-year, but for present purposes a conventional unit, say one year, may be taken for granted. Each process has a given labour input coefficient, a_1, which is then used to divide the other input coefficients, a, to yield a new vector, α, of inputs per capita. Thus α_{12} is the number of units of good 1 used per head in the production of good 2, the total input of 1 into 2 to be found by multiplying it by employment in 2. The output coefficient is no longer unity but rather output per head, or labour productivity, which, being multiplied by employment, gives total output. These relations hold for any quantity of labour, so that again scale and proportion may be separated by taking employment, e, as unity, i.e. $e = e_1 + e_2 = 1$. Productivity multiplied by price gives value produced per head and α multiplied by price gives materials cost per head. Labour cost per head is simply the wage rate, w. Likewise profit is per capita.

For each process input vector, a, there is an α. Depending on the labour productivity all inputs and outputs in a process are increased (or decreased) in the same proportion as is indicated in fig. 4.1. The effect all depends on productivity, but if we assume that it depends particularly on the inputs of the other good, then the locus of α's will have much the same shape as the locus of the a's but it will be stretched outward along its own axis, remaining convex. An equal stretching of the α's (e.g. by a profit rate) tilts the locus towards the axis of the other good and may increase its curvature.

This model is the same as that of Ch. 3 but expressed differently, and, if w be set at zero, the same results follow, though less conveniently. Reformulation is necessary in order to deal with different problems. Consider a stationary economy with a given technique, unit employment equal to labour force. The employment vector,

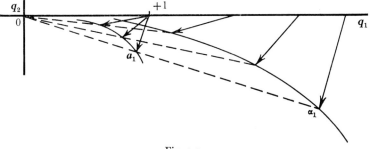

Fig. 4.1

e, in fig. 4.2 gives the proportional allocation of labour. If $e = e_1$ gross ouput per head is q_1 and net is u_1, and similarly for $e = e_2$. Any particular e attaches weights to q_1 and q_2, yielding q as their weighted mean. The same weights are applied to u_1 and to u_2 giving u, as well as to α_1 and α_2 giving α. With any price vector p, the materials cost per head for 1 is the projection of α, on p, i.e. lm; the wage cost per head is ow, the value of output per head is the projection of q_1, om, so that profits per head is the value less cost, wl.

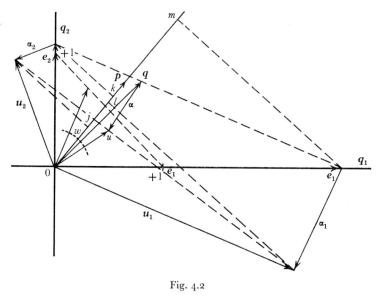

Fig. 4.2

The corresponding quantities for 2 are jk, ow, ok, and wj. There will only be competitive equilibrium if the ratio of profit to cost is the same in the two sectors. All this is independent of scale since the unit of labour can be 10 or 10 million, altering gross and net outputs correspondingly.

4.2. Distribution and production in the stationary state

Consider a stationary economy with all net product consumed; wages and materials are paid for in advance; interest and profit rate are equal; all pure profit has disappeared and operating profit covers interest cost; all rentier income is consumed. With a given profit rate and an initial set of prices (of unit length), each entrepreneur will choose that technique which will enable him, whilst covering all costs, to offer the highest wage rate. In fig. 4.3 the value of output (everything per capita) for industry 1 is oz, the cost of materials yz, with interest hz, so that a wage of ow_1 can be offered with $oh = ow_1 (1 + \pi)$, just exhausting the value of the product. A similar analysis of industry 2 leads to the offer of a wage ow_2. In a competitive regime this will lead to a reallocation of labour to industry 1 and a fall in its relative price. A counter-clockwise rotation of p will raise w_2 and lower w_1, gradually bringing them into equality. The projection on p of the vector u' gives value less materials cost, hence what is available for labour cost. p must rotate until the projection of u'_1 and u'_2 coincide. This gives a simple rule for determining the equilibrium p; it must be normal (perpendicular) to the locus of u'. It also locates the best technique, given the profit rate, which is the one selected by the common tangent to the locus of $(1 + \pi)\alpha$ for each industry. The best output being determined, its distribution is also determined, though not quite completely since the value of net output will depend somewhat on relative outputs.

Equally well w may be taken as given, then by gradually extending α and ow in the common proportion of $(1 + \pi)$, the solution is attained in which a line is tangent to the loci of both $(1 + \pi)\alpha$'s, and which has a perpendicular passing through the origin at a distance of $oh = (1 + \pi)ow$. The pair of values w and π will obviously be the same in the two cases, so that formally it does not matter which is taken as given. Thus given either w or π.

the other is determined along with relative prices, the best techniques, and the distribution of income.

The rate of profit, and hence the distribution of wealth, is
completely arbitrary; it may be anything from o to a maximum
value reached when u'_1 and u'_2 coincide, each normal to the same

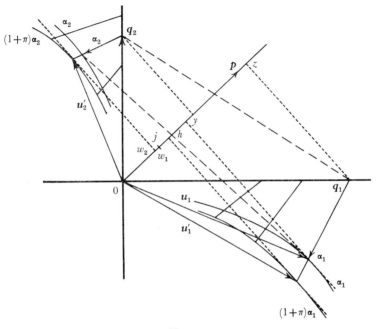

Fig. 4.3

price vector p, leaving wage rate and share of labour zero. It is a
striking fact that in an unchanging community, and many such
have existed and some still do, there is no reason why any existing
distribution of income should alter. This is, of course, subject to
some sort of lower subsistence limit on wages, but otherwise there
is no bar to any distribution no matter how extreme. This refers
to functional distribution, not distribution by size, though there
is usually a close connection between the two.

Not only is distribution arbitrary but so also must be, to a
limited extent, prices and the methods of production, as can be
seen from fig. 4.4. Begin with zero profit; the whole of net product
must be paid out in wages. Gross product, q, less inputs, α, is the
locus of u, net product. The price structure which gives equal

53

wage rates for both sectors and pays out the full value of net product regardless of its composition is the **p** normal to the locus of **u**. Then take higher and higher profit rates; these will hit harder those with higher materials cost, e.g. industry 1, so that to earn the same rate of profit and to pay the same wage, they must have

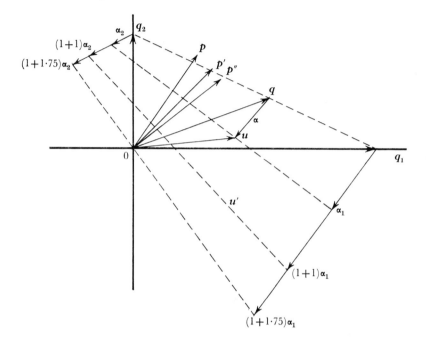

Fig. 4.4

a higher relative price. Cost of materials plus mark-up becomes $(1+\pi)\alpha$, and the locus of surplus available to pay wages plus mark-up becomes **u′**, e.g. $(1+1)\alpha$ in this diagram. There is only one set of prices, **p′**, which will enable both sectors to have the same mark-up and pay the same wage. Continuing with ever higher profit rate, the price ratio rotates until profit absorbs the whole product; the locus of **u′** passes through the origin; there is no surplus left to pay out as wages and **p″** is the only set of prices which will earn the same maximal profit rate for both industries. Prices, then, are free to vary between **p** and **p″** and are only partially determined by the available techniques, the final influence being distribution. The price ratio may shift, with an increase in profit rate, in favour of either 1 or 2; it will favour 1 if the slope of the locus of u from α_1 to α_2 is steeper than the locus of q, since this means it has the larger materials inputs. If the locus of u is shallower, then the materials inputs of 2 are heavier so that costs rise faster with a rise in mark-up and therefore prices shift in its favour, i.e. counter clockwise.

If prices vary with distribution the highest profit technique will also. The range of possibilities is great but the situation usually assumed is indicated in fig. 4.5. With higher and higher profit rates

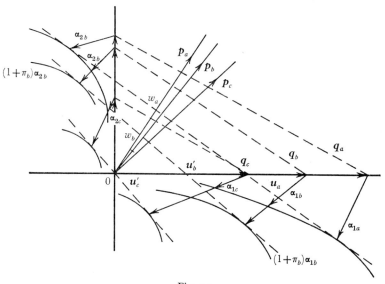

Fig. 4.5

the locus of u' is tilted one way or the other, e.g. to the south-west in the diagram. For any given wage the highest common profit rate is earned by the pair of techniques, e.g. α_{1b} and α_{2b}, determined by the common tangent to the loci $(1+\pi_b)\alpha$ which passes through the wage plus mark-up, $(1+\pi_b)ow_b$, thus also fixing p_b perpendicular to the tangent. Conversely, given π_b, there is only one set of prices which allows both sectors to pay the same wages, and these two techniques allow a higher wage than any other pair at that profit rate. The tilting of the loci along with convexity ensures that with increasing profit rate the best techniques move in toward the origin. The lower the wage the less productive is the technique chosen, the higher the wage the more productive.

55

The two extreme cases, zero profit and zero wage, are to be seen as two pure types of which all actual cases are a blend. Existing prices and techniques will lie either closer to or further from α_a and p_a as the profit rate is low or high. The same considerations apply to growth rates: p_a and α_a are the proper pair for a stationary state and p_d and α_d for the maximum conceivable growth rate, and to every growth rate in between there corresponds a price vector and a pair of techniques.

Since distribution affects the choice of methods of production, it concerns the shares in output but it also vitally affects the size of that output. When we say that α_{1b} and α_{2b} are the best techniques, it is to be understood that they are the best given the profit rate π_b or the wage rate w_b. They are not the best when the condition is removed. As the wage rate is higher and the profit rate lower, income is redistributed from rentiers to workers, but, in addition, net income is higher. The higher the wage rate the higher the locus of net outputs, u. The socially optimal result is obtained only if wages are pushed to their maximum, profits to zero, with net output possibilties given by u_a. This applies only to a stationary economy with zero growth rate. Along the line of u_a it is impossible to increase net output (consumption) of both goods without employing more labour than there is. Whereas for any other pair of techniques, including the 'best' ones given any wage rate below the maximum, it is possible to increase the net output of both goods by altering prices and techniques. Hence wages could be increased without lowering profits and vice versa, thus largely cancelling the effects of altering the ratio of wage-profit rates. This fits with the view that, given the required inputs of labour and materials, profit has no function, its sole justification, in both the short and long runs, being dynamic. In the short run its function is to reallocate supplies to achieve the correct proportions, and in the long run to accomplish the required growth in scale. Appropriately optimality requires a zero profit (and interest) rate, as Schumpter long ago maintained.

Yet in spite of this, the surprising and disturbing consequence is that there can be a long-run equilibrium at any profit rate up to its maximum. Once the maximum profit technique appropriate to any wage level has been attained, there is no necessary pressure for change even though consumption and net product are sub-optimal. No individual producer can gain by altering his methods and there is no excess or deficiency of labour to create any tendency for the wage level to change.

The Samuelson Substitution Theorem holds, i.e. no matter in what proportion goods are demanded, α_a techniques are best. Scale also does not matter; simply increase e, q, and u all in proportion and the optimal techniques remain best. Scale in the diagram, of course, need not be changed. By merely redefining the unit of labour, all possible net positive outputs can be accommodated to this one diagram, thus simply demonstrating universal optimality. If any positive net output can be produced at all (viability), all positive net outputs can, and they are best produced by a single, ordinarily unique, set of production processes. This is subject, naturally, to feasibility given the labour supply, i.e. net demand must lie within or on the triangle formed by the locus of u_a and the two axes. With optimal pricing and technique, and for this case only, the value of net product, $u \cdot p_a$, does not vary with the composition of output. The value of gross output varies with relative output. For any positive profit, the value of net product and, in consequence, distributive shares, will vary with the composition of output.

4.3. The labour theory of value

Why, in a stationary state, does only a zero profit rate result in optimal pricing? The simplest answer is that the net output line gives the rate at which good 1 can be transformed into good 2 through production and that the p perpendicular to it accomplishes the same transformation in monetary and market terms. By selling 1 at market price and buying 2, 1 is changed into 2 at the same rate as along u, since the money value of any set of goods along it is the same as that of any other set. Essentially goods 1 and 2 are not comparable; they are made so by the productive system because the output of one may be decreased thus allowing an increase of the other at some definite rate, say 5 to 1. A proper pricing system will then value them so that the unequal physical quantities become equal money quantities. At a deeper level the question arises as to how it is possible to make incomparables, say horses and cows, comparable. The answer must be operational: if, working at the limits of whatever it is that limits output, we can, by producing one less horse, produce five more cows, then, for what matters, five cows must equal one horse and they should be so priced. Here it is labour that limits production, so that the operative question is: if some labour be taken from 1 and added to 2, by how much will the net output of 1 be reduced and that of good 2 increased.

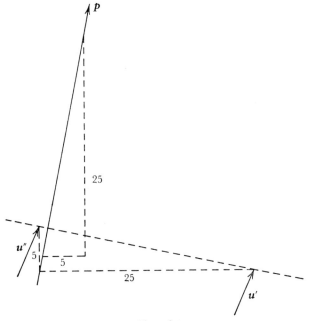

Fig. 4.6

Suppose, for example, that by transferring labour, 25 units of 1 are lost and 5 of 2 gained (fig. 4.6 u' to u'') then the price ray normal to the locus of u will have prices which are the inverse of the ratio of these quantities. If we say that the goods contain these quantities of labour, i.e. good 2 has 5 times as much as good 1, then the prices of each will be proportional to the amounts of labour in them. This is the labour theory of value, more or less the oldest serious theory of value, but one that is valid only where the proper conditions are fulfilled, as in this example. Take any pair of techniques, e.g. fig. 4.4, the price vector p normal to the net output curve, will correctly signal the productive possibilities of reallocating a given stock of labour. This is only so for a zero profit rate. If there is any positive profit, the corresponding prices, say p', will no longer measure the true results of reallocating labour and hence not measure the labour content of the two goods. By simple extension it is obvious that in choosing between techniques, the best choice will only be made if they are compared under conditions of zero profit rate.

4.4. Marxian value theory

The concept of economic surplus has no unique, clearly defined meaning; it means that it is defined to mean for the particular purpose in hand. The most fundamental one is that of net national product, i.e. gross product less what is required to produce it. The problem is: what is actually required to produce output and for whom. From the point of view of the social élite, labour is an input like another, surplus being gross value less cost of labour and materials. In fig. 4.5 it would be the difference between the value of net product u_b (on a line from α_{1b} to α_{2b}) and the wage rate. Since, in a stationary state, rentier income serves no productive purpose, it could be termed exploitation. It is exploitation in the sense that it could be removed by redistribution without damage to output. Yet there is a further, more subtle form of exploitation, not directly beneficial to the capitalist-rentier, but one which takes the form of inefficient methods of production, chosen as a direct consequence of levying a profit toll on output and thus introducing non-optimal prices. If a situation with maximum wage, w_a, be compared with one with w_b, but it is found that the workers gain more than the capitalists lose. The reason for the gain is the change to proper valuation by labour content.

Marx perceived that there was a basic contradiction between the fact of a surplus supporting a functionless élite, and the labour theory of value, a theory very common in his youth. He reasoned, quite correctly as we have seen in 4.3, that if everthing exchanges in ratios according to its labour content, there can be no surplus, the whole net product going to labour. Therefore, he concluded, labour must be the unique commodity that is paid less than its value, its cost of production in terms of labour, thus leaving something over for surplus. In this model labour is an unproduced input, with no cost in labour or anything else. However, suppose labour demands some real wage, whether subsistence or conventional, which gives it, like other goods a cost or exchange value. Yet, so long as this wage is less than its maximum, a rate of profit or surplus will arise. With such a profit rate, no good, labour included, is valued according to its labour content. Marx could have said that ordinarily labour content alone did not determine value and that in this way a surplus arose. Then he could have proceeded to say that the labour theory of value represented the ideal system for an economy, producing the maximum surplus for all members of the society rather than for the ruling class. To do this, however, would have required analytical tools not possessed by Marx or by any other economist of his time.

4.5. Wages, profits and the price level

The discussion thus far has proceeded on the basis of opposite variations in wage and profit rates: if the one goes up the other goes down. This holds if the price level is constant, but, alas, it rarely is. The actual relations of the two rates is richer and less definite. Take the situation in fig. 4.5; the wage and profit levels are arbitrary, which fits the classic trade union view that all that is required to alter distribution in its favour is to press hard enough for higher wages at the expense of profits. But is it so? This view ignores the commanding position of the capitalist producer in a capitalist economy. The wage is a money quantity, so that all the entrepreneur has to do is to keep his mark-up constant to retain his share at a higher price level, which will annul the intended increase in the real wage. In fact the higher wage is self-defeating by providing the higher level of demand necessary to sustain real demand at the higher price level. Prolonged full employment after the Second World War provided an ample demonstration of the reality of this hypothesis.

A fuller discussion of the price level is reserved for Ch. 6, but because of its crucial role in wage-profit behaviour, some consideration is necessary here. In the stationary state there are two simple, extreme cases between which lie a great number of mixed ones. The first one, which is the more significant and is the one considered in all the other sections of this chapter, is the analysis of what happens if the real wage is altered. The other case is what happens if the money wage is altered, the profit rate is maintained and prices are free to vary. Which, or what combination of the two, happens depends on the total situation.

Up to this point we have been able to enjoy the luxury of assuming a unitary price level, which made the value of a thing simply its projection on p. The complete statement is that the value of q, i.e. $q \cdot p$, is the projection of q on p multiplied by the length of p, which becomes essential if there is variation in the price level as

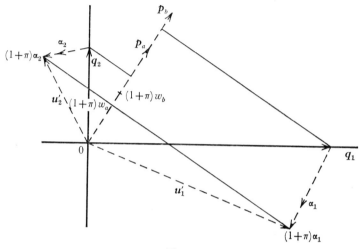

Fig. 4.7

measure by the length of p. Write $q \cdot p$ as $(q \text{ on } p)|p|$ where $|p|$ stands for the length of p. Consider an economy with a given technique and a fixed mark-up rate of profit, π, a price level p_a of unit length, and a marked-up wage of $(1+\pi)w_a$ (fig. 4.7). The value of good 1 is q_1 on p_a, its marked-up materials cost $(1+\pi)\alpha_1$ on p_a, so that the value available for marked-up labour is the first less the second, u_1' on $p_a = (1+\pi)w_a$. Similarly for good 2. What is the equilibrium effect of raising the money wage rate to w_b with unchanged profit rate? A solution is found by lengthening the p in the same proportion as wages, i.e. $|p_b| = w_b/w_a|p_a| = w_b/w_a$. Since the value of good 1 is then $q_1 \cdot p_b = (q_1 \text{ on } p_b)|p_b| = (q_1 \text{ on } p_b)w_b/w_a$, the value of output is increased in the same proportion as is the cost of materials, so that the value of u_1' is also increased in the same proportion and hence $u_1' \cdot p_b = (1+\pi)w_b$. Likewise good 2, though lower in value is also increased in the same proportion and $u^2 \cdot p_b$ is also equal to the new marked-up wage. A rise in the money wage has altered all prices proportionately leaving all real relations, including real wages, unaltered. It is an example of the 'monetary veil' doctrine that the real relations are unaffected by monetary or price level changes, and it is as secure as is that doctrine, which is to say, not very. It is to be particularly noted that here the real relations include a conventional mark-up and associated distribution of income which, in a stationary state, is completely arbitarary.

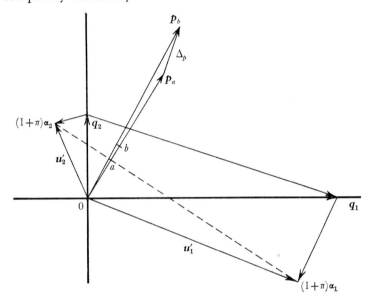

Fig. 4.8

Granted that such a solution exists, how might it come about? Suppose that the price of each good is formed by marking up by the given profit rate the costs of the previous period. Nothing essential is lost, and simplification gained, by assuming that each sector does not make secondary calculations by altering its costs to include its own intended price change. Given a general increase in the marked-up wage cost, each sector will increase its price only in response to the wage increase. As shown in fig. 4.8 the wage cost has gone up but $u'.p_a$ has not, and this deficiency, the same for both sectors, will be rectified by price increases. But the increase will not be in equal proportion because wage cost is a much smaller proportion of value in 1 than in 2. The value of good 1 output will be increased by the same amount as that of good 2, but, because of the higher productivity, the increase in p_1 will be in inverse proportion ot its productivity as compared with good 2. Thus $\Delta p_1 = (ob - oa)/g_1$ and $\Delta p_2 = (ob - oa)/g_2$, so that prices will alter in a direction perpendicular to the locus of q, not of u, p_2 rising more than p_1, because of its greater labour intensity and smaller dependence on materials. In the second period prices will continue to rise because now materials cost as well as labour

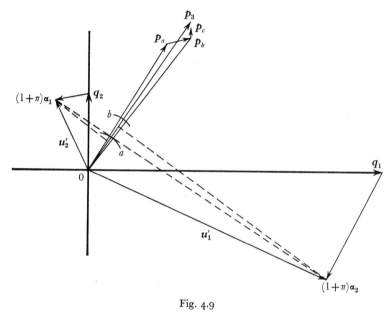

Fig. 4.9

cost has risen, but the scale of price increases will lessen since the value of u' for both sectors has risen towards ob due to the rise in the level of prices. However, since the value of u'_2 has risen more than that of u'_1, p will again alter direction, this time towards p_a. The level of prices will continue to rise as long as the value of either u' is below ob. The ratio of prices will continue to change until it has returned to its original ratio, for only then will the value of both u'_1 and u'_2 be increased by the rise in the general price level in the ratio ob/oa, when both will again equal the higher level, ob, of marked-up wages.

By virtue of its disaggregated nature, this model can simulate a basic feature of wage bargaining, i.e. wages are settled by industry not nationally. Suppose an equilibrium situation as in fig. 4.9 with unitary price level p_a, conventional mark-up π, and marked-up wage rate oa. Productivity is 2 in industry 1 and $\frac{1}{2}$ in industry 2. For whatever reason the wage is raised in 1 from $oa/(1+\pi)$ to $ob/(1+\pi)$, so that revenue fails to cover the profit rate in 1 by $ob-oa$. Next period p_1 is raised by $\frac{1}{2}(ob-oa)$ which will restore the profit rate, thus altering both price level and price ratio to p_b. Materials cost in 2 having risen, it fails to maintain its profit rate and will consequently raise p_2 by twice the deficiency, so that prices rise again, unequally, to p_i. This process will continue until a new equilibrim price vector, p_3, is reached, with the price level, p_3, increased somewhat less than the initial wage rise in 1. The condition that must be satisfied by prices is that

$$|p_3|/|p_a| = ob/(u_1' \text{ on } p_3) = oa/(u_2' \text{ on } p_3).$$

$|p_a|$ being unity for convenience; this means that the value available for labour, $(u_1' \text{ on } p_3)|p_3|$, is equal to what is required for the higher wage, $(1+\pi)ob$. Similarly 2 has just enough to pay its previous wage and earn the conventional rate of profit. To cover higher wage costs the price ratio has altered in favour of 1, which means u_1' on p_3 has risen so that the price level has risen less than the rise in wages in sector 1. Therefore the real wage in 1 has risen in spite of the maintenance of the profit rate, thus justifying their militancy. Though the workers in 1 have not achieved their aim in real terms, they have in real terms relative to their fellow workers, for the real wage in 1 stands in the same relation to the real wage in 2 as ob to oa. This example is well designed to bring out how, in our complex and interdependent economies, class conflict and sectional conflict become intertwined. When the workers in an industry get a wage increase they will ordinarily be doing so at the expense more of other workers than of their own or any other employers. The operation of the market tends to obscure the nature and results of these conflicts, but a century of education has brought class conflict into a fairly sharp focus, whereas sectoral conflict is only slowly coming clearly into view. It promises to be a potent source of social conflict in the future.

Although the workers in 2 are less militant or less favourably placed, they have experienced an actual, unbargained-for fall in their real wages. It is highly likely that they will react by pressing for and obtaining a rise in their wages. They may demand a restoration of their previous real wage (for this is a stagnant economy) or they may well be aware of what their fellow workers in I have obtained, asking and obtaining the same. In the latter event, a new process is started which brings first a rise in p_2, then one in p_1, then a bit more in p_2, and so on until the profit rate is restored without further rises in prices and costs. In the new equilibrium for both industries u on p equals oa, the money value is raised by the rise in the price level to equal ob, which is what is required for an unchanged profit rate. Both marked-up money wages now equal ob, but the rise in the price level reduces their real value back to square one, i.e. oa. These two processes may, of course, easily overlap in time. Subsequently it is the turn of the aggressive workers of I to react; they were first cheated of part of their gain by the first series of price rises; now they have been cheated of the rest of it, and so are likely to press for a further rise, and so on.

If real wages are to be raised the profit rate must decline, or else there must be a permanent inflation with a complicated redistribution depending on the speed of response of the two contestants. The difficulty lies in the question: what determines the profit rate? In this model it is arbitrary and hence might well be vulnerable to changes in the wage rate, but evidence from the more complex world of reality suggests that it is highly resistent to change in the long run. In any case it clearly does not follow that a change in the money wage rate will change the profit rate and indeed is rather unlikely to do so.

The converse problem is: what happens if the profit rate is raised with a constant wage rate and a price level free to vary. Each sector increases its price but in different proportions because of their differing cost structures. There are further rounds because of increasing costs as the prices rise. Not only does the price level rise but, in the final equilibrium, there is a different price ratio. The increase in profits is necessarily real so the price level must rise enough to reduce the real wage to the same amount as the money wage would have to fall with a constant price level. On the other hand if the attempt is made to keep the real wage constant by raising money wages, there is no equilibrium solution, as we know from the fact that in real terms if π rises the wage must fall. The result is continuing inflation with various possible redistribution effects depending on the reaction patterns of the two parties.

4.6. Capital as the time shape of production

This model can be completely specified and its behaviour studied without ever introducing the concept of capital, which is not one of its building blocks. However, profit does arise; it is a return on something called capital in a system called capitalist; hence it is desirable to attempt some analysis of what it is, how it arises, and it persists. It is significant that there is only one unproduced input, the factor labour, but there are two, not one, types of claim on net output—wages and profits. Unfortunately there are various meanings given to capital, and, worse still, its quantity, however defined and measured, is, unlike labour, not uniquely related to each process. Its quantity varies with its price (considered as the rate of profit) and, still more perversely, with the price of labour.

One meaning that might be given to capital is the quantity of goods required to produce any given output. In order to add goods to a single total, they must first be valued. For a stationary economy the whole gross output is necessary to produce the net output; its value is $q.p$. Given a particular composition of output, there will be a definite value of capital, which, for a constant price level, may be taken to measure the quantity of capital. Yet at different levels of π, the p vector rotates so that even for a given technique and a given gross output, the real quantity of capital varies with its own price.

Perhaps closest to commercial practice is the definition of capital as the total money outlay (with constant price level) that is necessary to produce a particular output. This is close to the previous one but is not the same except for a zero profit rate, because a rise of π means a transfer from workers to capitalists, whereas rentier income is not considered as a cost. Capital outlay may rise or fall because of the change in relative prices but this effect is overborne by the decrease due to the fall in the wage bill. Hence the quantity of capital varies with the price of capital.

66

Like many words in common usage, capital does not bear up well under close analysis. The Austrian concept of roundaboutness represents a bold and deep-going attempt to sort out the confusions engendered by this familiar yet elusive notion. Capital is to be regarded as simply a name for the pervasive temporal structure of all economies. There is no thing or group of things which is capital. Rather, inputs precede outputs and the pattern or time structure of this precedence varies between goods and processes. This fact is of great importance wherever growth is occurring and hence must enter into any price system or valuation which is used as a basis for decisions. Thus the deeper we probe into the concept of capital the more it tends to vanish into the earlier and the later, the temporal structure. To look for a thing called capital represents the fallacy of misplaced concreteness; there are no things called capital; there is only the dynamical interrelation or ordinary things, goods and labour.

To see this we may, by recursion, resolve a good into the labour that has gone into its making. A unit of, say, goods is made not by labour alone but by goods as well. In year zero a certain amount of labour is used along with given quantities of goods 1 and 2. In year − 1 these goods were in turn made by a quantity of labour and of goods. Add the labour to that of year zero, and carry the goods back to year − 2. Thus recurring backwards, we can find the total of all labour that has ever contributed to the production of a unit of 1. The process regresses indefinitely into the past or to the first bit of labour ever performed (as all living cells have a bit of the first cell ever to exist) but this need cause no trouble—after a short time the amounts of labour become negligible and the summation can be terminated with a good approximation to the full amount. The remarkable fact is that this sum total of labour will be approximately equal to the amount of labour required to produce a unit of net output of goods (and none of good 2). In this double, and reassuring sense good 1 may be said to contain this amount of labour. By an exactly similar process we can calculate the labour of good 2.

For zero profit rate, if we take this quantity of labour and multiply it by the wage rate we get the price of each good, so that the ratio of prices is the same as the ratio of labour contents, i.e. it is the labour theory of value. In stationary conditions it does not matter when the labour was used: if this year's output was worked on two years ago and the labour this year only yields fruit in two year's time, it makes no difference whether or not account is taken of this fact. Hence it is valid, in stationary conditions simply to sum all labour, whenever applied, to find the relative value of goods.

The trouble begins when there is a positive rate of interest. Whether there is simple or compound interest, the contribution to value of labour applied earlier will be greater than labour applied later, so that the labour content alone no longer determines value and price. Given a constant price level, a rise in profit rate will lower labour costs and raise capital cost, but it will affect differently two goods or two processes. The one with labour applied closer to the time of output will fall relatively to the one with labour inputs further in the past. This explains why prices must alter with a change in the wage and profit rates. The good with low labour and high materials inputs will have its labour inputs placed further back in time and hence will have a relative rise in costs as a result of a rise in profit rate.

For a given pair of techniques there is a unique recursive series of labour inputs, each good's series depending on the input structure of both goods. This time shape of labour inputs is the roundaboutness of production but there is no simple measure of it. Nothing short of the whole series will do since different profit rates will affect the different terms differently. Each labour input can be weighted by the time lapse to completion of the good to get a time average of investment of labour, but this will not give a usable single characterization of roundaboutness since variations in profit rate alter the weight of each different element of labour input. Thus this average period of production cannot furnish a measure of quantity of capital independent of the profit rate.

A numberical example is helpful in clarifying these points. Suppose the technique specified by input coefficients as follows:

$$a_{11} = 0 \cdot 2, \quad a_{12} = 0 \cdot 2,$$
$$a_{12} = 0 \cdot 4, \quad a_{22} = 0 \cdot 1$$

with labour inputs of $a_{l1} = 0 \cdot 25$ and $a_{l2} = 1 \cdot 0$ giving a labour productivity of 4 in good 1 and 1 in 2. Assuming price equal to cost and a unit sum price level, the wage rate must be $0 \cdot 433$. This productive structure gives rise, for unit output of each at time zero, to labour inputs which, being multiplied by the wage rate, yield the labour costs shown in fig. 4.10 for the first 8 preceding years. Summing these labour costs gives 0·414 for 1 and 0·567 for 2, both of which are close to the prices derived from purely current costs— 0·423 and 0·577. The difference between current and past labour costs is the size of the remainder to the beginning of time. A

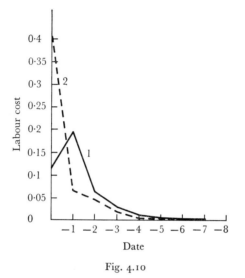

Fig. 4.10

better approximation is obtained from the ratio of past labour costs, 1·370 compared with the true value of 1·365. For good 1 the sum of past labour is 0·956 as compared with 0·978 currently required to produce one unit net. For good 2 it is 1·312 compared with 1·328. It is evident that good 1 requires a longer investment of labour than good 2, for, though it uses less labour in aggregate, it uses more in every year except the first. The average period of production of 1 is 2·65 years compared with 1·94 years for 2.

If the profit rate is raised to 50 %, the real wage must be reduced to 0·174. The lower wage reduces labour cost but interest charges raise them in a highly skewed way. Thus the wage bill in year − 2 is raised by over threefold by the time the product is finished, that in year − 5 over elevenfold, and in year − 7 over twenty-five fold. The combined result of these two influences is shown in fig. 4.11 which gives the labour cost with interest charges for each year for each good. The cost deriving from earlier years rise for both goods, but good 1, having the earlier labour inputs is more affected. The sum of labour costs for good has risen to 0·457 and for good 2 has fallen to 0·448, giving a cost and price ratio of 2 to 1 of 0·980, so that with the same productive structure 1 has become dearer than 2. A still more extreme case is shown in fig. 4.12 with

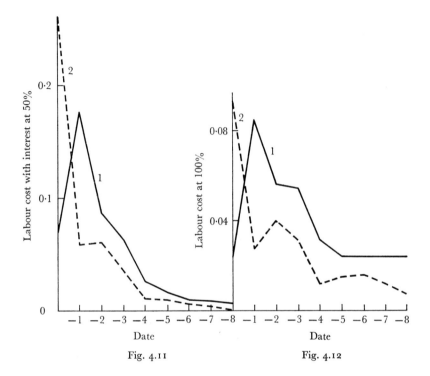

Fig. 4.11   Fig. 4.12

$\pi = 100\%$ and $w = 0·047$. The cost of the small, earlier labour inputs is raised even more, bringing about a price ratio of 0·716 between goods 2 and 1, so that good 1 has become much dearer.

As indicated in section 4.2, there are two pure or extreme cases, $\pi = 0$ and $\omega = 0$. In the example, for zero wage, π_{max} is 128 %, p_1 rises to 0·628 and p_2 falls to 0·372, giving a price ratio of 0·592. This limiting case leads to embarrassment; how can the goods be valued on marked-up labour cost when there is no labour cost? The answer is that it is not based on labour cost but on profits. Here we are back in the world of Ch. 2, and we can see clearly that what determines value is profits—a profits theory of value, parallel to, if not exactly symmetrical with, the labour theory of value. The value of output at time zero is profit per unit, Π_0, plus cost of inputs, γ_0. But the value of these inputs includes the profits on output in year -1. The value in year -1 includes cost in year -2 which in turn includes profits in year -3 and so on. Thus

$$p = \Pi + \gamma,$$
$$p_0 = \Pi_0 + \gamma_0$$
$$= \Pi_0 + \Pi_{-1} + \gamma_{-1}$$
$$= \Pi_0 + \Pi_1 + \Pi_{-2} + \gamma_{-2}, \text{ etc.}$$

Each regression brings lower costs and by indefinite recursion the cost element disappears and the price of each good equals the profits on all the past goods that enter directly or indirectly into it. It is to be remembered that these profits are uniquely determined, on the assumption of equal profit rates, for each sector by the input structures of both sectors. Hence, with zero wages, we may say that value is determined by the profit content of each good. This completes the picture of the two extreme cases, the one yielding the labour theory of value, and the other the profits theory of value, with all actual cases being various blends of these two pure types.

The labour theory of value is familiar, and indeed is quantitively the more important, but a profits theory of value sounds strange. Perhaps it is not altogether fanciful to envisage in the not so distant future an automated world with labour inputs reduced far below the labour force so that the most advanced economics return to a state like the most retarded with large unemployment. If a rational price policy is pursued, wages will be zero and prices will be all profit, the proceeds being distributed on any principle, welfaristic or power-controlled.

This approach may be generalized into a composite labour and profits theory of value. To produce a unit output of a good involves a labour cost, a capital (profits) cost, and a goods cost. The goods inputs, however, had to be produced in year -1, so that each year's inputs, of both goods, imply an equal value of outputs the year before. Thus, calling wage bill w per unit and Profits Π per unit.

$$\text{Value of 1 unit (Price)} = W_t + \Pi_t + \text{Inputs}_t,$$
$$\text{Inputs}_t = \text{Outputs}_{t-1}$$
$$\text{Value of Inputs}_t = \text{Value of Outputs}_{t-1}$$
$$= W_{t-1} + \Pi_{t-1} + \text{Inputs}_{t-1}$$

and so on indefinitely, so that we may write

$$\text{Price} = W_t + \Pi_t + \text{Inputs}_t$$
$$= W_t + \Pi_t + W_{t-1} + \Pi_{t-1} + \text{Inputs}_{t-1}$$
$$= W_t + \Pi_t + W_{t-1} + \Pi_{t-1} + W_{t-2} + \dots.$$

Thus recurring, each successive addition becomes smaller and eventually becomes negligible. Thus value is the sum of Wage and Capital costs regardless of when incurred, and for any one industry involves outputs and costs in both, according to the input structure. It is to be noted that this is net output, since none of it is involved in the inputs. The successive pairs of outputs are the same as those in the dated labour resolution; the difference being that there the labour cost had to be raised by profit rate to get profits cost, whereas here it is kept as dated profits.

$$p_1 = {}_1W_0 + {}_1W_{-1} + {}_1W_{-2} + \dots,$$
$$+ {}_1\Pi_0 + {}_1\Pi_{-1} + {}_1\Pi_{-2} + \dots$$

and similarly for p_2. The labour cost consists of the required output in each sector times the labour coefficients times the wage rate. The capital cost is the rate of profit times the required capital outlay in monetary terms. Capital outlay consists of wage bill and value of inputs of goods. Thus, though costs of materials each period is shifted backwards to previous costs, they are retained in the value of capital stock.

Capital outlay may be called 'capital', even 'real capital', allowing for the constancy of the price level, so long as it is understood that it is merely a name for a collection of heterogeneous quantities, having no independent existence of its own, quite unlike labour. With this proviso, we may write

$$\text{value} = wL_1 + \pi K_1,$$

where L_1 is the sum of the labour requirements and K_1 of the capital outlays for all the earlier outputs necessary to produce the required inputs for a unit output of 1 and similarly for industry 2.

The K thus defined is unavoidably a value, not a physical quantity (and hence π is a pure number not a quantity with dimension like w), and it includes wL_1 along with the total value of all inputs required. Hence the quantity L is unaffected by changes in π, w or p. By contrast K will completely change with alterations in π, w, and p.

An advantage of this formulation lies in the fact that, by netting out all goods inputs, the time structure of inputs is made irrelevant so that the problem of value, distribution and capital can be treated in current, timeless form. Taking everything in per capita terms, the problem can be fully visualized from fig. 4.13. For zero

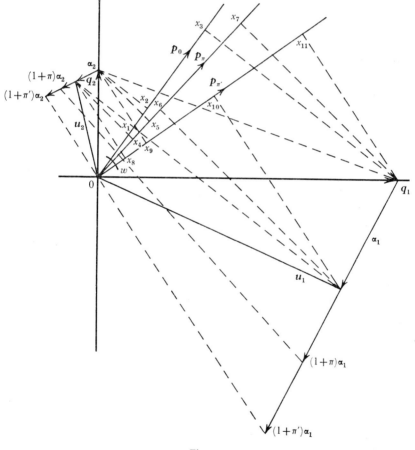

Fig. 4.13

73

profit rate, equilibrium prices, p_0 must equate the value of net output, $u.p_0$, with one another and with the wage rate $w_0 = ox_1$. The share of wages in net product is unity in both sectors. Though there is no income from capital, there is a quantity of capital, the whole value of gross product, ox_3 for 1 and ox_2 for 2. Of more significance than this unit capital gross output ratio is the ratio of capital to net output, ox_3/ox_1 for 1 and ox_2/ox_1 for 2. Taking the numerical example discussed above, capital per capita, K_1, is 1·69 and K_2 is 0·58 which gives a capital output ratio of 3·90 in 1 and 1·33 in 2.

With a positive profit rate, π, the wage falls to ow, and the price of 1 must rise relative to 2 to cover the higher capital cost of 1, so that the price vector rotates from p_0 to p_π. The quantity of capital in 1 is $ow + x_6 x_7$ and in 2 $ow + x_4 x_5$. Capital in both sectors has fallen due to the fall in wages. Due to the alteration in prices, net value output has risen in 1 to ox_6 and fallen in 2 to ox_4 with the result that in both the capital output ratio falls but more in 1 than in 2. In the numerical example, with $\pi = 50\%$ and $w = 0·174$, $K_1 = 1·37$ and $K_2 = 0·33$, net output in 1 is 0·86 and in 2 0·34, so that the capital output ratio in 1 has fallen to 1·59 and in 2 to 0·97. The share of wages in net output in 1 is 20·3% and in 2 is 51·7%. These all hold for 1 unit of labour used in sector 1 or sector 2, and need only alteration of scale for any size employment. Any actual output will consist of both sectors and the aggregative result will lie closer to the one or the other depending on the composition of output and the consequent allocation of the labour force. Thus these wage and profit rates, the capital output ratio can vary between 1·59 and 0·97 and the share of labour between 20% and 52%.

As there are higher and higher profit rates, the price of one with the heavier goods inputs rises and so does its net value product. Invested capital decreases in both, and, in the limit with maximal profit and zero wage, the capital invested in each becomes simply the cost of goods inputs, $x_{10} x_{11}$ for 1 and $x_8 x_9$ for 2. Since net output is then entirely profits and the profit rate must be the same for both, the two capital output ratios are equal and equal to $1/\pi$. The share of profit is equal to unity in both. In the numerical example maximum profit rate is 128%, which reduces capital in 1 to 1·10 and in 2 to 0·16. With a net output in 1 of 1·42 and in 2 of 0·21, which gives a common capital output ratio of 0·78.

This analysis shows how complex, even in the most simplified model, is the problem of capital. To begin with there is no identifiable capital; it is merely a word to describe an aspect of the temporal structure and functioning of the economy. It refers to the sequence of inputs and outputs that must precede any net output, the greater the capital, the greater the 'tail' of necessary outputs stretching backwards in time. Or, looked at a moment of time, this greater capital intensity shows itself by a greater input of goods, a greater difference between net and gross output, and, in the diagram, by the steeper slope of the net as compared with the gross output line. In the example sector 1 uses more capital than sector 2; it has a higher capital to labour ratio, K, and a higher capital to output ratio (except for maximum π). There is a given technique in each industry hence no marginal products or possible substitution between labour and capital. The results hold for any quantities of labour, if sufficient inputs are available. Yet the higher is the profit rate, the lower are the capital labour and the capital output ratios in both sectors. These effects are primarily due to the redistribution if income and, in particular, to the lower wage rate.

Do these results make economic sense? Output is limited by two things labour and material inputs. If labour is the limiting element, the wage should be high and profit rate low, which will increase the capital labour and capital output ratios through the high wage bill. Secondly, the use of 1 will be encouraged and of 2 discouraged because of a low p_1 compared to p_2. If there is substitution in consumption this will shift labour and output allocation to 1 which has high goods inputs and low labour inputs, thus being appropriate to shortage of labour as compared to goods. This effect will be much greater where there are alternative techniques allowing for substitution in production. The rationale of the wage effect on capital is that wages lead to consumption before output whereas rentier income only accrues after the output is available and only leads to consumption, if at all, after the output is available.

If, by contrast, production is limited not by labour but by the pre-existing goods necessary for inputs, then pricing should favour low wages and the output of goods with small inputs of goods. This means that 'capital' is scarce, the rate of profit high and wages low, which will make the capital–labour and capital–output ratios

75

low, thus reducing inputs relative to output and gaining the greatest output from the available goods. Also the price of 2 will be low relative to 1 thus shifting output more to 2 from 1 with saving of goods inputs or 'capital'. Capital represents the goods necessary to undertake any level and composition of output and includes two distinct parts, the goods input and the wages bill, here assumed to be entirely spent on goods. Thus it is evident that all this can be described without mentioning 'capital' but that it can also consistently be described in terms of capital intensity. In the stationary state, whatever the situation, there exists a set of prices which will equate wage and profit rates in different sectors and thus give a possible equilibrium. With no net saving and no tendency for wages to alter, the temporal structure and hence capital is of no operative significance and hence irrelevant. For dynamics it is vital and this aspect requires further discussion.

4.7. Distribution and production in a growing economy

Received doctrine on capital accumulation, fragmentary and inadequate though it is, might go somewhat as follows: positive saving leads to a gradual increase in the stock of capital; output increases but the rate of interest falls. A clear picture of the process can be obtained by a careful study of fig. 4.14, representing an economy with a constant spectrum of three techniques for each sector, and a constant labour supply. There is a competitive money market with rentiers supplying a slowly increasing quantity of money capital and of the goods represented by it. The economy is poor with output a weighted average of q_1 and q_2 and a wage of oh $(1 + \pi)$. The entrepreneurs may wish to use the highly productive techniques α' or α'' but in attempting to borrow the funds (and hence the goods represented by them) they inevitably come up against the fact that the α technique does not produce enough output to supply the inputs of α'. In consequence they bid up the rate of interest (to about 100 %) until it leaves just enough to pay wages. At this high rate of interest both α' and α'' would result in losses. As net saving continues, the larger quantity of capital will only be taken up at a reduction in π. With lower π the entrepreneurs enjoy a transient profit which they dissipate in bidding against one another for the constant labour supply. Thus with a given technique, the quantity of capital rises through the rising wage rate. If the wage rate were to rise to about $oh'/1 + \pi'$, the profit rate would have nearly disappeared, but before this dire result happens, it becomes more profitable to shift to α_1' or d_2' or both. At a wage of $oh'/1 + \pi'$ with the new technique α_2', the profit rate has only to fall to about 30 % instead of to zero. There ensues a gradual shift from α to α' techniques, but this process of

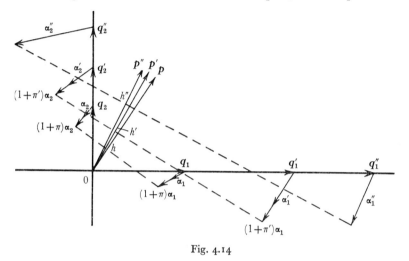

Fig. 4.14

accumulation is quite different from the previous one. Here the savings of rentiers go, not to increasing real wages and lowering real profits, but to increasing real inputs and outputs. Once the transition to α' has been completed, then capital accumulation will again take the form of altering the distribution of income. With a given technique a rise in the share of labour means less real income for rentiers, but with rise in productivity this need not happen. The profit rate is lower but the amount of capital is greater; the share may be lower, but it is a share of a higher output. The real income of labour must go up but that of rentier–capitalists can go either way. As drawn in fig. 4.14 it has stayed about constant. This alternation between the rise in output and in wages is unreal, due to the small number of discrete processes, but it does serve to separate out clearly two quite distinct aspects of capital accumulation; the increase in goods required for higher wage and increase in goods required for higher inputs in production. As the

77

two sectors will not have equal productivity gains there is bound to be a shift in relative prices, from p to p', to benefit the less productive sector. The wage rate rises by more than oh to oh' since $w' = oh'/1 + \pi'$ and π' is lower than π. At this wage rate, the most productive technique, α'', would yield a lower rate of profit than α' and hence at an interest rate equal to π', would produce a loss. Finally, suppose the wage rate is pushed to its maximum value $w = oh''/1 + \pi''$. Even with no interest cost, entrepreneuers would experience a loss with α' and be forced to alter methods to the more productive α'', with a resulting shift in prices to p''. This is clearly the social optimum with a unique set of prices, but valid for any output whatsoever so long as it is feasible with the given labour force. Any positive profit is sub-optimal in the sense that, by a change of technique, the rentiers could be paid the same income whilst raising the income of workers. There would be a transitional period required to accumulate the larger inputs of goods, but the wage could ultimately rise and remain at the higher level indefinitely. Any of the sub-optimal positions is consistent with a maintenance of long-run competitive equilibrium, given zero saving, in spite of clear knowledge of more productive alternatives.

This fact is presumably central to the explanation of some of the semi-stagnant underdeveloped economies. The rentiers consume rather than save their incomes, with the result that the economy settles down to a unique long-run equilibrium of low wage, low productive techniques. No pressure for change is likely to come from the labour market since it is chronically depressed because of excess supply.

In the nineteenth century some such analysis was the basis for a widespread belief in the necessity (law) of an ultimately falling profit rate. It might not fall rapidly due to low saving; it might take an unconscionably long time because of the possibility of falling back on these ever more capital using techniques and on high wages. How fast and how far were less clearly envisaged. If the rate of interest controlled the rate of saving, then it would fall to that rate at which there were no further net savings. If, however, saving depended, even only in part, on the income of rentiers then this suicidal slide would continue to ultimate extinction, though it would become very slow in the later stages and never actuallly be completed. Always implicit, but not always explicit, in this analysis were the twin assumptions of small or non-existent growth in both labour force and technology. Since both were high throughout the period, it is difficult to see much usable content in the law. Harrod and von Neumann changed all this by showing that with a growing labour force (and/or technological progress) there could be perpetual capital accumulation with no necessary fall in the profit rate.

4.8. Full employment growth

If the economy has a steadily growing labour force, at rate g, then an optimal solution requires full employment and full employment requires the accumulation of a part of current output both to expand the means of production and pay in advance the wage bill of the larger labour force each period. As in Ch. 3, to find the per capita inputs out of last period's output, the input vectors, α, must be lengthened to $(1+g)\alpha$. Thus if an output $\bar{q}$ per head required 0·5 good 1 and 2·5 of good 2 per head, an output now of 1·10 requires 0·55 and 2·75 respectively. The loci of α_1 and α_2 (in fig. 4.3) uniformly stretched give a new, somewhat more curved, pair of loci. The greatest possible consumption now lies anywhere on a straight line tangent to the two stretched curves $(1+g)\alpha_1$ and $(1+g)\alpha_2$ in fig. 4.15. The unique optimal prices will be normal, p^*, to this line. These outputs from last period can, however, be used to employ a larger number of workers with consumption of $(1+g)c$, c being consumption per head and gc representing an advance to workers on output that will only accrue next period. The value of total consumption is $oh = (1+g)\,ow$, ow being value of consumption per head. The value of investment per head is $(gc+gd)\cdot p^* = wk$, the value of net output ok will be equal to the value of consumption plus the value of investment, i.e. $c\cdot p^* = (gc+gd).p^*$. The optimal techniques a_1^* and a_2^* will ordinarily be different from what they would be for a stationary labour force. Yet no other technique can be found which would allow higher consumption of both goods. This optimal solution has characteristics that are an amalgam of those for a nil wage and those for a nil profit rate, depending on how large g is.

It is quite impossible for managers to find the solution and impractical for central planners to do so. However, if managers set the wage rate at ow, maximize the profit rate = the interest rate, with zero pure profits and prices equal to costs, they will have the optimal prices and techniques. The wage bill, which is independent of relative outputs since $l_1 + l_2$ is given and the wage rate is the same for both sectors, will equal the value of goods available for consumption (likewise independent of relative outputs). The

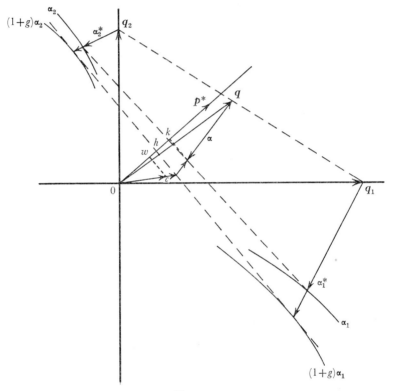

Fig. 4.15

remainder of net income, interest income, must then be used to finance accumulation and correspond to the value of investment, $(g\mathbf{c} + g\mathbf{a}).p^*$. Any other combination of wage and profit rates will sub-optimal, permitting an increase in the consumption of both goods.

This result, that optimality with steady growth requires profit rate equal to growth rate and profits equal to saving and investment has come to be called the Golden Rule because it makes consumption as great as possible subject to the growth rate. It is a direct consequence of von Neumann's analysis with the difference that, whereas he took consumption as given and maximized growth rate, here the growth is given and consumption is maximized. The solution will be the same in both cases. There is an important difference in that, with a given consumption pattern, a particular eigenray of output is determined, whereas if we start with the eigenvalue (growth rate) there is a free choice of consumption pattern and hence growth ray of output. The equality of profits and savings is independent of whether any, all or none of the profits are saved and invested. The amount of saving is determined but who does it is another matter; it could be done in part or wholly out of earned income, or by taxation or on any other principle.

Because wages make up a different proportion of costs in the two sectors, the relative distributive shares will vary with the composition of output. Only if wages take all is labour's share constant, with alterations in relative outputs. In fig. 4.15 c is consumption, $g(c+d)$ investment, and the projection of $c+g(c+\alpha)$ on p^* is the value of net product, ok. If output q were to be different, ok would be different but not the value of c. Profit is $ok-ow$ and since neither the wage, w nor wl, the wage bill, changes, this means that profits per head does change and hence its share changes. In spite of changes in distribution, the optimal technique remains so regardless of what relative, and also absolute, output is. Therefore the Samuelson Substitution Theorem remains valid and there is only one best technique of production, so that input–output analysis, with a single set of input coefficients, is also valid.

Evidently there is an intimate connection between growth rate and profit rate. In the past the relation was viewed as a looser and indirect one, acting through the interest rate and acting equally on all incomes, earned and unearned alike. A subtle and complex theory of rational action was constructed on the basis of maximizing the satisfactions of present and future consumption. The complexity of the theory is so great that it is difficult to find empirical confirmation or negation of it. It has many defenders and attackers, but one central point counted heavily in its favour;

it was held, following Bohm–Bawerk, that a pervasive preference for present over future consumption was necessary to explain a persistent positive rate of interest. Since almost all economic analysis was of a stationary economy this view had much to be said for it. But the moment we take a dynamical standpoint, the reverse proposition is nearer the truth—a positive rate of interest is necessary to explain the example above, growth can go on

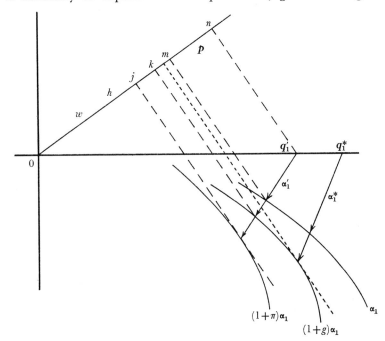

Fig. 4.16

forever, with supply of and demand for investible funds both increasing in step, so that there is no need of scarcity or psychic balancing at the margin to explain a positive growth rate and interest rate.

By contrast with this elegant and insubstantial theory of time preference there is a crude one, without much rationale, but one which is very well supported by fact. Savings, particularly for industrial and commercial expansion, come largely out of the profits of private and public companies. Furthermore, happily for the theoretician, there seems to be some tendency for these savings to be a constant fraction of profits. Suppose, then, that a constant proportion, θ, of profits is saved, and, for simplicity, that no labour income is saved. Further assume that an equilibrium is established, without looking too closely at how or whether, such an equilibrium is established. The required growth rate, g, is given and achieved. With a proportion, θ, of profits saved, capitalists' income has to be large enough to yield the required saving, i.e. $\theta\pi = g$, since both π and g are applied to cost of materials and of labour. As shown for sector 1 in fig. 4.16, maximizing profit rate means choosing technique α_1' as contrasted with the optimal solution α_1^* with $\theta = 1$. The value of gross product is on, and of net product om. Of this net product the wage cost is ow, and profits wm. Out of profits hk is consumed; $wh + km$ is invested, wh in labour and km in materials. As we have seen optimal behaviour requires $\pi = g$, but here profit rate is greater than growth rate with the consequence of sub-optimal pricing and choice of technique. With these prices a_1^* is optimal providing a higher set of possible consumptions, so that either capitalists or workers or both could consume more. Perhaps even more serious is the result that the apparently un-related and innocuous institutional decision about the value of θ determines in large measure the distribution of income. The smaller θ is the larger must be the share of profits and hence the lower the share of wages. Therefore any consumption out of profits not only lowers the net product but distorts in an arbitrary way the sharing of that smaller product. Thus a large θ, corresponding to a high profit retention rate, is doubly beneficial to labour; it gives labour a larger share of a larger product.

4.9 Maximum growth rate with no scarcity of labour

The previous section gives a good vantage point from which to get a better appreciation of exactly what was von Neumann's problem and its solution. Essentially it is the same as that of the previous section except that he reversed the order of causation. He assumed that the real wage was given and maximized growth rate. This implies that labour force growth is open to choice. Such a condition is rather special but could be found in an industrializing economy which could draw any amount of labour through immigration, including internal migration from a totally separated subsistence economy of some sort. The given wage can be a subsistence wage, a conventional wage or the wage necessary to attract an unlimited supply of labour, but it must be independent of the rate of immigration. Before employment the labourers are no charge on the economy, but from the moment of employment, they must be supplied with the wage goods and the inputs required by the adopted technique. The problem is the same as treated in fig. 4.15 except in reverse.

In consequence of the argument of the previous section, it becomes clear that the, at first sight surprising, assumption of von Neumann that all profits are saved and all wages are consumed, was not made for analytic convenience or because most saving is in fact done out of profits. It was made because maximizing either the wage rate or the growth rate, given the other, requires optimal choice of technique and this will only occur in a market mechanism if $\pi = g$ and that is only likely to happen if all profits, and only profits go into accumulation. To see this, construct a diagram as in fig. 4.17. The given wage rate is indicated by a circle about the origin, along with gw to allow for the increment to the labour force; the two sets of technical knowledge are the loci of the vector, α. Now expand all three curves along their respective rays by a small proportion g and continue, taking ever larger g's until it is possible to draw a common tangent to all three curves. This is the von Neumann optimal solution; g cannot be made any larger without perpetual run-down of stocks. If this wage is paid and these prices set, the profit rate will equal the growth rate g. If workers spend their entire receipts, their demand will just equal net consumable output, no matter how they spend it. Any other pair of techniques would yield a lower growth rate, given the wage rate. The price vector is unique but the net and gross output vectors are free for choice. Once the workers have set their pattern of consumption c, this determines the q^* necessary to produce it and this defines the perpetual growth path of output and employment —the von Neumann ray.

It is also shows that given w, the von Neumann price ray and eigenvalue are unique, but the workers' basket of goods can be anything (substitution theorem), and that only when it is set, is the quantity ray determined. It is easy to trace in the diagram the effect of alterations in the pattern of consumer demand. The allocation of labour and productive resources would be shifted in the same direction, but the remarkable fact is that the growth rate would be totally unaffected. Given optimality the single determinant of growth rate is the level of real wages. With a subsistence wage, the growth rate is unique. But if the wage rate can be above subsistence, then the growth rate can vary from a maximum value to zero. For poor countries this range may be pitifully small. In fig. 4.17 draw the common tangent of the w circle and the locus

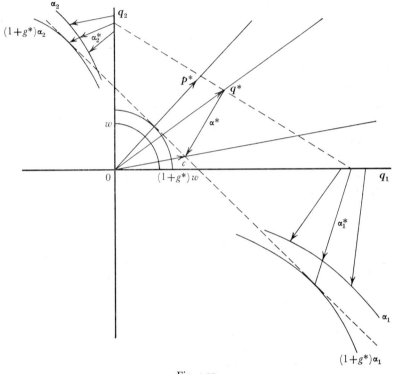

Fig. 4.17

of α_1 (not $(1+g)\alpha_1$), and do the same for α_2. If these two straight lines intersect at an angle of less than $180°$, the economy is viable, if at more than $180°$, not viable, and if they coincide, it is the limit of viability.

In spite of the dazzling brilliance of the von Neumann analysis, an analysis which has helped to set the whole generation of economists to rethinking basic concepts, there are some unsatisfactory aspects. This growth which is maximized is simply the most rapid proliferation of near misery, as if one were to set about

85

unrolling an endless slave economy on a deserted continent. This is growth in a very narrow sense and it can be doubted whether such growth is desirable. What has attracted economists to von Neumann is not the details of his model but the high power of his theoretical apparatus.

Consider the case, surely much commoner than the von Neumann one, of a country with a large body of unemployed who are supported, through some sort of familial redistribution, out of the wages of those fortunate enough to be employed. What should an ideal, all-powerful central planning board do? By contrast with the previous case with its constant cost of labour, there is no cost of labour; it is a fixed or 'sunk' cost, and as such should not enter into the production decisions. The paradox of von Neumann's model is that though labour is not scarce, in the sense that its supply is infinitely expansible, it has a constant cost. Assume that the aim of the board is to maximize growth rate (a more sophisticated aim will be discussed in Ch. 7), whilst maintaining constant the average consumption of the whole labour force, employed and unemployed. The population can be growing at any rate λ so long as λ is less than the achieved growth rate of employment g.

In such countries, in spite of massive unemployment, it is common to find that there is an operative minimum (and for homogeneous labour, maximum) wage rate. It would be natural, though strictly illegitimate, for the planners to identify this wage with the von Neumann given wage, and proceed to maximize growth rate. This would, if they succeeded, produce the solution of fig. 4.17, i.e. p^*, α^* and g^*. Unemployment would be reduced at the rate $g^* - \lambda$; the average consumption would rise. This solution, though no doubt better than will ever be achieved in practice, is, however, not optimal.

The error lies in taking the wage rate as given, when, in reality, it is not given. Thus, if employment were to be increased, the wage could be lowered whilst still maintaining the same average consumption. What are really given, are the outputs of last year, the total labour force, known techniques, and the total consumption $\bar{C}$, but not the wage. The aim is to increase output as rapidly as possible without using more goods than there are available from the previous year's output. It is easier to use the Ch. 3 type diagram with inputs per unit of output, but with outputs and consumption on an absolute scale, as in fig. 4.18. Ignoring transient problems of getting outputs in the right proportion, the solution is obtained by extending the loci of α_1 and α_2 in a common proportion until their common tangent passes through $\overline{C}$.

This chooses the optimal technique, a^*, prices, p^*, normal to the tangent, and determines the maximum growth rate, g^*.

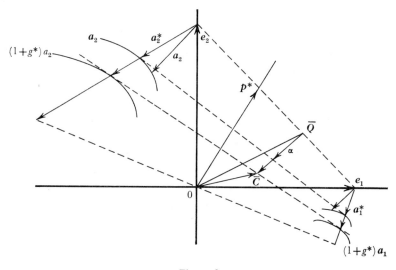

Fig. 4.18

The techniques will be different from the technique chosen by taking the conventional wage and solving a pseudo-Neumann problem. There may be more or less employment than with the conventional wage, presumably more, but it is unlikely that the amount of employment will add up to the labour force. The state extracts $\overline{C}$, or its money value $\overline{C}.p^*$, from the surplus and distributes it equally amongst employed and unemployed, the remainder of the surplus going to supply growth inputs. The next period output is up by a factor g^*, consumption by λ, or, to keep to a constant scale, consumption can be considered as going down by $g^* - \lambda$, so that g^* can be increased next period. Thus keeping the same technique, there is a gradual acceleration of g, quite contrary to the behaviour in the pseudo-Neumann case, where a best g is chosen and remains constant throughout. The acceleration continues until full employment is reached, at which point, average consumption must be¦ suddenly raised, and the growth rate pushed back to λ (fig. 4.15). This course of action, keeping consumption at its existing level and then suddenly raising it to its maximum is unsatisfactory and surely sub-optimal when considered over the whole sequence of events. A fuller treatment of this difficult problem is reserved for Ch. 7.

4.10 Summary view of distribution

The simple picture is that those who labour should receive the whole product of their labour, i.e. wage take all. But in a stationary economy there may exist any wage between subsistence and one equal to per capita net product. The purpose of this analysis is to show the possibilities, the setting of the problem, rather than to give much indication of actual wage–profit determination. In practice it is extremely difficult to alter an existing real wage; inflation is the like result. What the existing wage is may perhaps be explained in each particular case.

The introduction of dynamics somewhat reduces this arbitrariness. With some given growth of labour force, the whole product is not available for consumption either by workers or capitalists. If capitalists consume $\frac{1}{2}$ the profits the profit rate must be twice the growth rate of labour force and output. This is a semi-stationary state, i.e. output and employment grow but technique, output and consumption per head are unchanged.

Real wages can rise if profit rates fall, but this seems unlikely to happen if the initiative is from the side of workers. This conclusion is strongly supported by the evident failure of profit rates to show any tendency to long run downward drift, for which the model provides some explanation. If the workers do succeed in pushing up real wages, accumulation falls behind the growth of labour force, weakening the bargaining power of labour and, in any case, reducing average consumption. In these conditions they are unlikely to be able to resist a rise in the price level in relation to money wages, thus restoring the profit rate. On the other hand if prices rise more than money wages, raising the profit rate, accumulation rises so that output and employment grow faster than the labour force. Employers bid against one another for the increasingly short labour force, resulting in rising real wage and falling profit rates. The induced, gradual transition to less labour intensive techniques slows the fall but cannot stop it. As the profit rate and capitalists share of output falls, accumulation ceases to keep pace with the rising labour force, the pressure on the labour market eases off, and real wages cease to rise. Thus we see that the profit rate cannot be too high, nor can it be too low and that indeed it must be approximately constant (with constant growth rate of labour) in the long run.

Now add technical progress to the picture. It may mean lower labour inputs, or lower inputs of goods, or both, or more inputs of goods with less of labour, but whichever, it means, in the first instance, a rise in profits over the market rate of return. But this means increased saving, an urge to grow faster on the part of producers which will lead them to bid up the price of funds and of labour, so that the pure profit is dissipated in higher interest and wage rates. Once the transition to the new techniques is completed, the high profit rate yields a higher growth rate of output and employment so that there will continue to be pressure on the labour market with a tendency for wages to rise until the profit rate has sunk back to its original level, with wages high enough to have absorbed the whole of the rise in productivity.

Technical progress consists of a large number of small events, partially, though not wholly, independent. The consequence is something like a steady rise in productivity. Profits are continually arising only to be cut down. Not only this but with more output and input per head, the total flow of goods must rise faster than the labour force; the rate of growth of output is rate of growth of labour force plus rate of growth of productivity. Hence the long-run rate of profit is a multiple of rate of growth of output, not merely of labour force growth.

The argument supports the view that it is productivity which, in combination with a given behaviour pattern of capitalists, regulates wages, not the other way round. This is subject to an important complication. Technical progress is specific; it occurs at one time in one industry. Profits go up and accelerated expansion is possible and desirable. To achieve this with full employment means setting up a wage differential. The other industries are then under pressure to raise wages to hold their labour forces even though productivity has not risen. To do this they must shift to more labour productive techniques. Here wages are determining productivity, not the converse. Further adaptation is, however, required. Higher wages and higher productivity in the unprogressive industries means a lower profit rate, so that long run equilibrium will require a rise in their prices and a fall in those of the progressive industry, raising profit rate in the one and lowering it in the other.

4.11 A digression on surplus value and how to build pyramids and palaces

The underdeveloped countries of the world can only undertake very modest programmes of development because the poverty of the people means that only a small proportion of their low output can be saved and invested. At the same time in some such countries one can see vast piles of masonry, ruins of temples, palaces, fortresses, etc., and one can imagine the scope of the ghostly armies of soldiers and servants that once serviced these earlier societies. An insistent question arises: how could these people, very near the lower limits of human existence, out of whom only very little in the way of savings or taxes can be extracted, how could these people ever have borne the burden of building and manning these complexes? On the assumption that productivity was not greatly higher than in the backward economies of today, how was it possible to accomplish all those Roman Works, the roads and aqueducts, the baths, forums and ampitheatres, or the Valley of the Nile, the cathedrals and courts of medieval Europe, or the Mogul palaces and fortresses, or the temples of Central and South America?

Keynes, with characteristic insight, first noticed that these may not have been built by the sacrifices of the populace, as popular history has it. His suggestion was that the theory of effective demand put it in a new light, suggesting that these public works programmes may have actually benefited the peoples. Unfortunately we now know of, what Keynes did not know of, the pervasiveness of a different sort of unemployment in the underdeveloped economies—an unemployment not caused by a lack of effective demand not one curable by public (or private) spending. Although the explanation of this situation is not very clear, it is fairly safe to assume that it was not radically different in the past.

These countries are primarily agricultural; their output is mostly from the land and is limited by the amount and character of that land. The amount of arable land is variable but only within narrow limits. With a best technique of cultivation there is also a limited amount of employment. In such a situation we may rephrase Malthus as follows: subsistence is that level of consumption which raises deaths to equal births in a prolific community; a level of consumption above this leads to expansion of work force but not of employment until the average level of consumption (of employed plus unemployed) is reduced to subsistence; thereafter a stationary state exists. The amount of unemployment is a measure of the surplus or degree of viability of the economy. Each fully employed person produces a product, some fraction of which is required for himself and necessary dependents (wives or husbands, the old and the young). The difference between output and subsistence is a measure of the surplus produced. The Malthusian resolution is that average consumption tends to subsistence, so that we get:

labour force × average consumption = employed × average product or

$$\frac{\text{labour force}}{\text{employment}} = \frac{\text{average product}}{\text{subsistence}} = 1 + \text{Rate of Surplus}.$$

Thus the ratio of labour force to fully employed workers is a crude measure of surplus.

This puts an altogether more favourable light on the possibilities of conspicuous waste in past civilization. The rate of surplus thus measured can scarcely ever have been less than 15 % and must often have been as high as 50 % or 100 %. This means that, say, one person in three is available for public works at no reduction in the standard of living. It takes a ruthless power machine to accomplish such a task, but these regimes were never lacking in ruthlessness.

How such a regime did in fact carry out this sort of mobilization must be largely guess work, but there is an economic analysis which may provide a clue. If those who work are taxed heavily and the proceeds used to employ those who do not work at the subsistence wage, the net result on consumption, total and average, is nil. The taxes impoverish and the spending enriches so that the one cancels the other with no change in consumption. Output, however, goes up by the value (such as it may be) of what is built or serviced by the newly employed. Income before taxes goes up but income after taxes remains constant. This is known as the Balanced Budget Theorem and is of great importance in financing modern wars—our own form of conspicuous waste. The newly employed in ancient times had to be in armies, in building and construction, or personal service or state pomp or religious functions—all occupations separate from agriculture which could absorb no more employment.

Viewed in this light, it is seen as a matter of social organization. Once the regime is overthrown or decays, the lavish expenditure ceases, the taxes cannot be collected and the villages again have to support a large, mostly useless, surplus population, which is, apparently, the normal condition of pre-industrial economies.

4.12. Unequal steady growth rates

In reality there are never equal growth rates, primarily for various reasons excluded by assumptions only be to relaxed in a later chapter, e.g. the rise in per capita incomes and technological change. To show how unequal growth rates can be handled, assume that, along with a given growth rate, g, of labour force, there is a steady change in the consumption pattern. Furthermore, suppose that this rate of change is correctly foreseen and that the economy effects an equilibrated response to the steady change.

Problems arise the moment we leave the artificial paradise of equal growth rates. Optimality requires, given the growth rate in the labour force, a common profit rate equal to this growth rate and a highest common wage rate. But here growth rates must be unequal to maintain the equality of supply and demand. Therefore either the equality of profit rates is sacrificed or their equality with growth rates goes and in either case optimality is lost. However, by virtue of the substitution theorem, prices, wage rate and best technique are independent of output. Evidently it is not the different demand patterns but the transition from one to the other that causes the trouble.

In a planned economy, given the rate of growth of labour force and hence of the economy, if full employment is to be maintained, the highest common rate of profit will be equal to the growth rate and the wage rate is thus determined along with the relative prices that yield the common profit rate along with the best techniques. Then keeping the techniques and wage rate, but not the profit rate, each industry is instructed to grow at such a rate

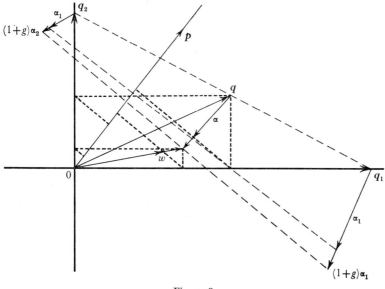

Fig. 4.18

as to keep supply equal to demand and to set prices so as to earn a profit equal to its particular growth rate. They may even adjust their individual wage rates as widely as is necessary to achieve the necessary re-allocation of labour. The result is non-optimal prices but so long as there is no alteration of techniques, no harm is done.

This has a very Marshallian flavour to it. If the over-all growth rate be associated with normal profits, then the high growth industries have high profit rates and the low growth (or even declining) ones have low profit rates. If the rate of interest equals the over-all growth rate, some industries will have pure profits and others pure losses.

An important question is whether and to what extent there must be reallocation of investment funds. If all profits are saved and invested, in aggregate there will always be just enough savings out of profits to finance the investment. For the case of equal growth rates each industry will have exactly enough funds to cover its investment, no matter what output is, as is shown in fig. 4.18. Therefore complete retention of earnings would provide automatically the funds required for investment. Is it also true for unequal growth rates, or must there be a redistribution of funds through a capital market or government agency? Some inspection of fig. 4.18 will show that no matter what growth rates are, and regardless of outputs, the projection of any point on the line from $(1+g_1)\alpha_1$ to $(1+g_2)\alpha_2$ will divide the value of last year's output into two parts, one of which is the cost of this year's goods inputs and the other of this year's wage bill, so that receipts will always cover outlays including investment outlays $g\alpha$ and gw.

In an unplanned economy, the persistence of unequal growth and profit rates can have two unfavourable effects. It will lead, in the effort to maximize profit, to choice of sub-optimal techniques and it may lead to excessive or deficient transfer of resources from one industry to another, for, in the absence of complete plough-back of earnings, the transfer of resources depends on the responsiveness of entrepreneurs. This might be considered as a cost of attaining the necessary adaptation. It is, however, just conceivable that a perfect market might achieve the same result. With no uncertainty profit rates could tend to equality under condition of sufficient flow of funds from low to high growth industry.

5

DURABLE GOODS

5.1. Adaptation of the model to include durable equipment

The analysis of the time structure of production becomes immensely more complicated where there are goods used more than once, durable goods. In order to elucidate some principles it is necessary to make further violent simplifications of the same sort as those already incorporated in the model. With a known and constant technology, one sector, h, produces goods as previously, but the other, e, produces homogeneous units of equipment which are used by both sectors to produce current output. Equipment includes, besides machinery, such things as buildings, roads, wiring, piping and furnishings, etc., i.e. all goods that are used more than once.

Repeated use creates the problem of allocating the cost between the various years. Durable goods, rather like human beings, do not have a definite life-time but rather a statistical life expectancy. Their productivity is likely to decline with age and their maintenance costs to rise. These difficulties show up in the calculation of the depreciation charge, which, along with interest cost and maintenance, represent the cost of a machine for a year. Although depreciation is basic to all commercial practice, its distribution over the years is to some extent arbitrary.

A piece of equipment is envisaged as gradually imparting its value to the goods it helps to produce until, with luck, at the end of its life, it has yielded up all its value in the form of output. Thus the value or capital locked up in a machine gradually falls to zero, so that, on the average, the value of equipment will be around half its price new, even though it may enjoy substantially constant productive capacity to the end. On the other hand a collection of machines will usually suffer a number of deaths differing from year to year, with the result that the value of the group diminishes to zero, but, in this case, so also does its productive capacity. Fortunately these two quite different cases behave in much the same way in a nearly steady state with no rapid

95

accelerations or decelerations. If there is a constant relative death rate, θ, then with any number of machines, x, θx will disappear in one year. Happily the quite different case of a steady state with a steady number of machines installed each year, each machine lasting $1/\theta$ years, results in a disappearance of θx machines each year out of a population of x machines.

Making the assumption that θ units disappear each year, regardless of age, and ignoring maintenance costs, the current cost of a piece of equipment is the interest cost in its price plus the depreciation, i.e. $(\pi + \theta)P_e$. Although some such formula is widely used in practice, the most that can be said in its favour is that it is extremely simple and easy to use. This is the long-run equilibrium cost of equipment once in existence and it is to be sharply distinguished from the cost of producing it, which, in equilibrium, is simply its price.

The model, then, consists of a flow of perishable goods and of equipment, each currently produced with both as inputs along with the services of a stock of labour and of equipment. As in Ch. 4 it is convenient to take inputs and outputs per capita of labour employed. Each process specifies a labour input per unit of output, a_1, which is then unity, but also an equipment input, a_e, which is then α_e, machines per capita. The current flow of machines required to sustain this output is $\theta\alpha_e$. The outputs per man, q_e and q_h, depend vitally on the equipment per man ratio, α_e, and hence on the current input, θa_e. The resulting structure is very similar to that of Ch. 4 except for the fact that productivity in e depends on its input of e, not as in Ch. 4, on its input of h. This means a marked asymmetry in the locus of the input requirements as shown in fig. 5.1.

The assumption of a homogeneous output of durable equipment is peculiarly unfortunate, however necessary for exposition. In reality there is, of course, a great number of industries producing high differentiated types of equipment, each quite incapable of producing other products. Some account of this can be taken by assuming that once a piece of equipment is produced it is no longer homogeneous and must be used in the process for which it was designed. An example is the brick industry which produces a sufficiently uniform product but which becomes embodied in a myriad of different structures, from simple to complex, with a great variety of functions. Once it is 'fixed in its form, it may, for practical purposes, never be used for any different purpose. Many other examples have been mentioned, e.g. timber, steel, plastic, electronic components, but, alas, there is no universal equipment good, such as is embodied in the model.

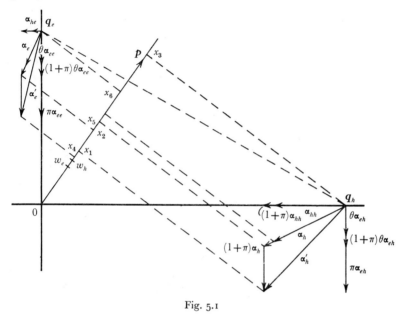

Fig. 5.1

The main difference from Ch. 4 is that 'fixed' as well as working capital has to be considered. In fig. 5.1 there are two given techniques and a given price vector and profit rate. For h the capital equipment is α_{eh} (not shown) which leads to a current cost of $\pi\alpha_{eh}\cdot p = x_1 x_2$. Current working capital is the value of α_h, which with interest cost is $(1+\pi)\alpha_h\cdot p = x_2, x_3$. The balance of working capital is in wages with $(1+\pi)\, w_h = 0x_1$, giving a total outlay equal to the value of the product $0x_3$. Similarly for e, working capital with interest is $x_5 x_6 + 0x_4$ at a wage w_e. Fixed capital charge is $x_4 x_5$ with total current outlay exhausting the value of the product at $0x_6$. The problem is to find a p which will equate w_e and w_h for the given profit rate. w_h being higher than w_e, h can attract labour from e, expand output and precipitate a price fall until $w_e = w_h$.

In equilibrium p must be perpendicular to a line from α'_e to α'_h; an increase in π will lengthen the two unequally and hence require an alteration in p. At zero π the wage will absorb the whole of net national per capita income lying on the line connecting α_e and α_h. As we consider higher and higher profit rates α' will be projected further and further below α, tilting the line connecting the α's one way or the other thus altering relative prices and lowering the real wage. π_{max} is reached when this line passes through the origin with all net national product absorbed by profits. The quantity of capital varies inversely as π increases, primarily due to the fall in w, the working capital invested in wages. The remainder of capital is the projection on p of $\alpha_h + \alpha_{eh}$, if only h is produced. In any actual case the amount of capital will be a weighted average of these quantities for the two industries. As π alters so do prices thus altering the value of a constant stock of goods and equipment. The addition of durable equipment serves to strengthen the point that there is no identifiable entity capital and that it is rather an aspect of the over-all functioning of the economy.

5.2. The spectrum of techniques in the very long run

The early capitalist economies effectively faced a rather narrow range of techniques to choose from and this is still true of the developed economies. By contrast the underdeveloped economies are in more or less full possession of an enormous range of techniques more productive than their present ones. Often they cannot take advantage of these techniques because they do not have the equipment nor the industries to produce it. It is, nevertheless, of considerable interest to assume away this difficulty by supposing that their durable goods industry can produce any type of equipment. The problem of accumulating the equipment in advance of use is ignored in this section. Basically it is a problem of using a range of ever more complex equipment to use (and/or thwart) natural forces, primarily energy, to do what otherwise has to be done by man himself. Human energy is replaced by natural energy, controlled by means of the equipment. Human energy has remained until recently necessary to control the processes, but even this vestige is disappearing with the development of cybernetic control mechanisms.

Labour productivity is taken to depend essentially on the

stock of durable equipment in use. Although it is not necessarily so, it is assumed that with increases in equipment per head, output per head goes up but less than proportionately. The per capita input of goods, h, is taken to be roughly proportional to output per capita. The input of equipment in durable goods may be either greater or less than in perishable goods, but to bring out the particular characteristics of the model they are taken to behave similarly. An example based on these assumptions is given in fig. 5.2. Since current replacement is a constant fraction, θ, of equipment stock, this one datum can be used for both quantities, keeping in mind that the stock is $1/\theta$ times the flow. The fact that equipment determines productivity in both sectors means that as θe increases, the input vector of h inclines ever further away from its own axis whereas that of e does the opposite. The consequence is that the locus of $\boldsymbol{\alpha}_e$ tends to be pressed towards its axis whereas that of $\boldsymbol{\alpha}_h$ splays out from its axis. The base of the vertical component of $\boldsymbol{\alpha}_h$ is output per capita in function of the input of equipment per capita. $\theta \boldsymbol{\alpha}_{eh}$. Its slope is the marginal productivity of equipment and the slope of a ray from the origin to any point on the locus gives the output equipment ratio.

In the very long run the optimum choice of techniques is determined by the common tangent to the two loci of the $\boldsymbol{\alpha}$'s, giving the largest net outputs possible regardless of the composition of demand. The profit rate is zero and wages absorb the whole product. More productive techniques may exist in both sectors but the added equipment requires more labour for operation and replacement than is saved, quite apart from the initial accumulation of the equipment.

The corresponding price vector $P_{\pi=0}$ values each good according to the amount of labour embodied in it; thus the very long-run social optimum requires the labour theory of value, and in particular that equipment be valued according to its labour content.

By the methods of section 5.1 the effect of any common profit rate can be found. The profit rate may be anything from 0 to the maximum given by the common tangent which passes through the origin. As larger and larger profit rates are taken, the loci of the extended $\boldsymbol{\alpha}''$s shifts downward but also alters slope in such a way that the highest common profit rate is earned by utilizing less and less equipment. The locus for roughly a 30 % profit rate is show in fig. 5.2, with a resulting different choice of technique, set of prices, $P_{\pi'}$, and wage rate w'. In a stationary state, any distribution of wealth is possible, but a rise in the share of profits not only reduces the share of labour, but also the size of the product

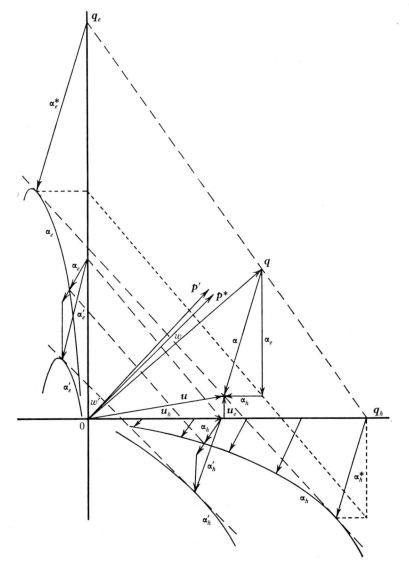

Fig. 5.2

being shared. The same analysis applies to maximum growth rates in employment and output.

The same diagram can be used to determine the required inputs of equipment and of goods. Thus in fig. 5.2, for the optimal technique, given a demand u for net output, gross output must be q and $q - \alpha = u$. Net output of perishables is u_h, and their use as raw materials is α_h. The stock of goods on hand at the beginning of the period must be enough to supply replacement of consumer durables u_e and of producers' durables α_e. But these flows of replacement are proportional to the stock of equipment which must be in existence at the beginning of the period, i.e. $l(u_e + \alpha_e)$.

5.3. Distribution and value with given technique

Consider an economy with a single given technique in each sector as in fig. 5.3. The inputs per capita are given by α_h and α_e. Exactly as in section 4.6 the output of each sector can be separated into labour and goods, the goods here being perishable, h, replacement of equipment, e. These goods were in turn produced a year earlier by labour and goods and thus recursively the time structure of labour inputs required for each good can be derived. The sum, for each sector, of these labour inputs regardless of timing gives the total labour input and their ratio is represented by the price vector, p, normal to the line connecting the two input vectors. The effect of positive rates of profit is to inflate the earlier applications of labour relative to the later ones. In general this will alter relative prices but it is not obvious which price will be raised relatively, since both goods are used in each process. The effect on cost can be obtained directly from the extended α, i.e. α'. The difference between α and α' is interest cost and its value is its projection on p. Illustrated in fig. 5.3, is a profit rate of 20 %; one of 10 % would be $\frac{1}{2}(\alpha' - \alpha)$ and one of 40 %, $2(\alpha' - \alpha)$. If, as is the case here, the projection of $(\alpha'_e - \alpha_e)$ on p is greater than that of $(\alpha'_h - \alpha_h)$ this means that the time structure of labour inputs is slanted towards earlier years, and hence the addition of a compound interest charge has raised the cost of e more than it has for h. Therefore for equilibrium with price covering cost including an equal profit rate, P_e must rise relative to P_h, i.e. p rotates towards the e axis. Current wage cost per capita, with and without interest, is the same for both sectors and hence may be ignored. The equilibrium unit price vector, p'', for $\pi = 0.20$ is the normal to the line connecting α'_h and α'_e. The important consequence of this is that the value of any given stock of equipment has been raised in the most important sense that when it comes to be replaced it will cost more. The value of inputs of raw materials, h, will have gone

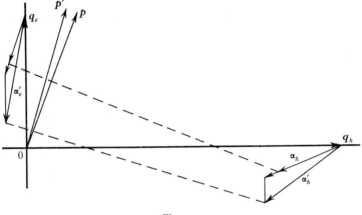

Fig. 5.3

down, but since equipment is normally more valuable than raw material input, the value of material capital will have risen. That part of working capital constituted by the wage bill will necessarily however, have gone down. The condition that there is no change in the price of equipment is that $(\alpha'_h - \alpha_h) \cdot p = (\alpha'_e - \alpha_e) \cdot p$. If the projection of $\alpha'_h - \alpha_h$ on p is greater than the other, then its price must rise relatively. This relation of profit rate to relative price is often called the Wicksell Effect after its discoverer. If $(\alpha' - \alpha) \cdot p$ is the same for the two goods, wage cost plus interest declines at a constant rate with increasing π. In all other cases it changes at a varying rate, which makes for complications.

The Wicksell Effect has theoretical importance greater than may at first be evident. Let the complications of working capital be ignored as being of lesser quantitative significance. An unchanged physical stock of equipment may have a different value, even at a constant price level, with every rate of profit. If labour is applied earlier in the instrumental trades, the 'real' value of equipment is higher, the higher the rate of interest. In the other case it is lower.

Only in the improbable case of an equal time structure is there a direct relation between real capital invested and quantity of equipment.

Although there is no strong presumption that a rise in π entails either a rise in costs of e relative to h or the converse, there is no doubt of its effect on both sectors. Given the assumption of the declining marginal productivity of equipment, the slope of the locus of the α's increases as higher and higher rates of profit are considered. The heavier the usage of equipment, the greater the input of goods in output and hence the earlier is the implied input of labour, and hence the greater the effect of any rate of profit. Therefore the greater the profit rate, the heavier the penalty on the intensive use of equipment in both sectors. Hence regardless of the relative intensity of equipment, in each sector, both sectors will want to use less equipment per unit of output the higher the rate of profit (*vide* fig. 5.2).

5.4. The accumulation of equipment in step with output and employment

Growth in output is separable into two components, growth in output per head employed and growth in employment, all actual growth being some mixture of the two. Both require the accumulation of stocks of goods both perishable and durable, the latter being quantitatively much larger. Though per capita growth is more important, growth in employment at constant per capita inputs and outputs is the only one simply analysable and to it we now proceed.

Increasing employment, inputs and outputs is running to stand still. Each period a larger stock of consumables, raw materials and durable equipment must be assembled prior to the next period's production on an enlarged scale. Yet next period consumption, inputs and outputs and equipment are all the same per capita. It is this fact that allows one diagram and one solution to stand for an accumulation process of unlimited duration. Formally the analysis of a common growth rate is the same as that for the timeless profit rate. For any given growth rate, g, the required current inputs are given by α', and the input of raw materials by the projection on this horizontal axis and the gross accumulation on the vertical axis (fig. 5.3). The formal similarity hides a real difference however. When output is resolved into dated labour inputs, π represents a skewed weighting or valuation. Whereas with growth, the α' represents actual production at an enlarged scale including new equipment. Therefore if this productive situation is resolved back into labour, the greater g is the greater is the actual outlay of earlier labour rquired.

Given any growth rate of labour force, which it is required to equip and employ, the range of possibilities can be represented by fig. 5.2 with g substituted for π. The common tangent to the loci of the α''s gives the locus of consumption vectors larger than any others possible with the same growth rate. Thus it exemplifies the Golden Rule in a Golden Age of constant growth rates—the highest maintainable consumption given the growth rate. This one solution represents any number of successive years with each year's labour force being taken as unity with outputs and inputs per head remaining always the same. This is called the widening of capital, ever more of the same types of equipment, techniques unchanged. If there is unemployment, any growth rate greater than that of the labour force may be chosen so long as the effect on consumption is tolerable or desirable. In principle, if not in practice, the greatest growth rate (nil consumption) can be chosen.

Suppose for the moment that equipment is present in whatever quantity is necessary. Employment is required to grow at the maximum rate consistent with a given wage rate and maintaining a constant level of machines per man, which means not only providing for replacement of producer and consumer durables but equipping the newly employed with the same quantities. No profit and all wages are consumed.

The problem is to find what growth rate will require current usage just to equal last year's outputs, q_{t-1}. A given wage, w, leads to a particular pattern of consumption, c, for an output of q. At last year's employment, per capita demand for h would have been C_h so that current demand will be $(1+g)C_h$. The demand for consumer durables (housing, etc.) will be for larger replacement and a new addition to stock thus giving rise to a growth demand of $(1+g)C_t$ plus g times the stock of consumer durables, transforming C_t into C_t' as shown in fig. 5.4. If only h were produced, it would require current perishables of $(1+g)\alpha_{hh}$ and replacements plus new additions to stock given by $(1+g)\theta\alpha_{eh}+g\alpha_{eh}$, and similarly for e. Therefore if q_{t-1} has been produced and production and employment is expanded in the correct scale g and in the same proportions, the total productive inputs are α' and consumptive uses are c' and they just exhaust the outputs available from last year.

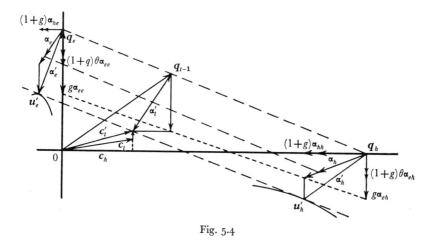

Fig. 5.4

By expanding c' and the locus of u' with increasing g's we eventually come to a locus of u's the common tangent to which passes through c'. This determines the techniques (and prices) which will yield the greatest possible growth rate per capita given the wage rate. This will be recognized as the von Neumann problem, and is a blend of the two extreme types of nil wage rate and maximum wage rate. Any other technique would require, to maintain the same growth rate, greater outputs than are available. Any other relative outputs would likewise lead to imbalance in supply and demand.

The growth rate need not be that of the labour force; by taking larger and larger growth rates, the relation between employment growth and consumption is revealed and allows of a choice on the basis of some further criteria. For each rate of growth, there will be a different price vector, which represents the labour required to sustain this growth rate including the new equipment required for the expanding employment.

If the producers save and invest all their profits, and if they maximize the profit rate and if profit rates are brought into equality, then the best technique, the right prices, and the correct allocation of resources for any given growth rate of employment will have been chosen. If only a part of profits are saved, π is greater than g, output is reduced and the reduced output is redistributed in favour of profit takers.

5.5. Growth in output per capita through the accumulation process

Full employment growth at a constant rate is all very well, but, at the end as at the beginning, it leaves most nations with a very low level of output and equipment per head. The urgent problem is to increase output and equipment per capita, but just at this point the problem itself becomes vastly more complex and this for a number of reasons. Durable goods by the very fact of their durability always exist in quantities large with respect to their annual output. Thus the stock in use at any time can only be increased or decreased over a considerable period. It is the existing stock of durable equipment that binds most economies to a very low level of output. It is tempting to say that it is a high profit rate that makes a low productivity technique most profitable in under developed economies, but it may well not be so. In any case it is the shortage of equipment which sets the level of productivity however this works out.

The optimal behaviour can no longer be stated straightforwardly in terms of a single year since the level of consumption and saving in one year affects output and hence consumption in later years. Therefore optimal solutions require statement in terms of behaviour over a number of years, strictly an infinite number of years. But obviously this makes an enormous complication. An introduction to the problem is given in Ch. 7.

In terms of productive structure the analysis becomes much more difficult. The behaviour of the economy in any one year is used, in part, to alter the very structure of the economy itself. It is, so to speak, laying its own track as it goes, but for this very reason it is much more difficult to plot a course for it. No single graph will do as in the case of a constant per capita growth. Not only this but, again, durability causes complications. If we produce equipment correct for the optimal techniques in one year, it will still be there some years hence, when, the structure of the economy now being different (more productive, more intensive types of equipment), it will no longer be optimal. Therefore no decision about best technique can be made in terms of one year alone. What is worse a number of different types of equipment and of techniques will be in operation at the same time.

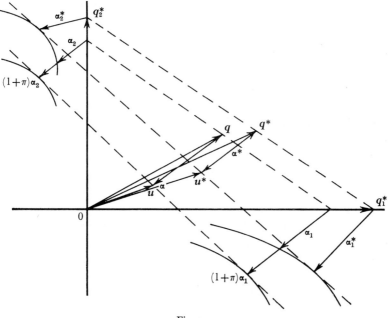

Fig. 5.5

Consider first the accumulation process for an economy of perishables only, both because it is simpler and in order to emphasize the difference with the case of durables. In fig. 5.5 the stocks of goods available at the outset are q, being the output from a fully employed and constant labour force. The long run optimal position depends on the consumption pattern with rising per capita consumption, say u^*, with output q^*. If producers adopt the α^* techniques with zero profit and proceed to hire all the workers their demand is for α^* and the workers is for u^* and the two add to q^* which is greater than the actual stocks q. Bidding up the prices of the goods in itself alters nothing since only relative prices count. Various sequences are possible. The producers may get the required inputs but consumers only bid up the prices and receive $q - \alpha^*$ and next year ask for and obtain higher money wages with inflation continuing. However, the inflation produces profits. But with a positive profit rate, the most profitable techniques becomes less input intensive. Alternatively the shortfall in goods may be shared between producers and consumers with the result that production is undertaken on a smaller scale with some unemployment resulting. In this case the bargaining power of workers is weaker and they may not be able to push up wages in step with prices thus leading to a fall in real wages and a rise in the profit rate, so that the best technique again moves towards α from α^*. Or the producers may restrict originally their scale to the available inputs with massive unemployment. If this leads to a fall in real wages, the techniques will be altered towards α, with more employment at lower wage rates. Thus by various routes the economy is likely to arrive at the equilibrium position of output q, input α and consumption u out of wages. If the resulting high profits are consumed this unsatisfactory distribution of income achieves a restriction of usage of goods to existing supplies but at a heavy cost in social justice. However, if some or all of profits are accumulated as an addition to available stocks of goods, then the equilibrium makes more sense, for the object is, or should be, to progress from q to q^*. Each year the available stocks increase and q moves outward, so that each year, either stocks are unsold leading to a fall in price (and rise in real wages) or all the stocks are purchased but entrepreneurs cannot find enough manpower to produce so that they bid up wages and profits gradually fall. The most profitable technique creeps outward towards a^* and consumption out of wages rises towards u^*, q moves towards q^*.

There are two principal differences between this accumulative process and the same situation with durable goods as well. The accumulation of equipment out of current output allows of only an advance in scale of a fraction, θ, of the added equipment, and it is therefore a much longer and more painful process. Secondly, whereas homogeneous raw materials can be totally changed in use each year from one process to another, equipment is ordinarily specific to each technique. Therefore one cannot creep along from technique to technique—only the gross increment of new equipment can be adapted to the newer more intensive, 'deeper' techniques. The result is that during the process there will be an array of bits of equipment corresponding to a whole series of techniques lying between α and α^* and hence production cannot be represented for the two techniques α_1 and α_1^*, as a weighted average of the two and the resultant input vector will lie somewhere, depending on the proportions of equipment, on a straight line connecting the two actual input vectors.

5.6. Rapid accumulation in a planned economy

Underdeveloped economies face a very different situation from that which the early capitalist countries faced. These economies gradually developed more productive techniques but at any one time there was a narrow range of more productive techniques available. A country now undergoing industrialization faces a vast range of techniques and it has a difficult decision. Its choice of technique is limited by the small amount of equipment it has at any point of time. Should it therefore utilize very unintensive techniques, spreading it thinly over many workers, or should it use the highly labour productive techniques used in developed countries? One thing is clear there is no question of spreading any existing equipment since that is 'fixed' in its present, presumably, low-productive form.

The problem, then, is about in what form to 'fix' the new productive equipment. The quantity of this new equipment will depend on many things, especially on the available equipment in the equipment industry. If the economy was previously stationary, than the full capacity was taken up in replacement and the total supply of new equipment would be the annual industrial replacement. This implies the gradual running down of the traditional industries through failure to replace. Whatever the situation, the available new equipment would be total capacity output less what was necessary to replace consumer durables (though a considerable run down might be tolerated as in war time). In reality, of course, much of this is irrelevant since the existing equipment industry can produce little of any industrial use, but this requires a vastly more complex analysis. The amount of equipment available may be determined by the purchasing power of the available export surplus of some primary products, but this is excluded by hypothesis.

Proceeding with the assumption that the equipment industry can as well build palaces as hovels, the most sophisticated automatic machinery as well as the simplest hoe, in what form should it produce equipment? Suppose that the aim is the most rapid (not the same as optimal, *vide* Ch. 7) transition from the existing low level labour productivity to the optimal labour productivity. The Samuelson Substitution Theorem cannot be used because that goes in terms of one best technique expanding indefinitely. But here we cannot attain the best technique, and expansion with the existing, attainable technique locks the economy forever in poverty. Fortunately the linearity assumed means that the model can equally well be used to discuss the whole economy, or any increment to it, the same proportional inputs and outputs applying to both. Hence with the available gross addition to equipment, there is completely free choice of technique, the scale on which it is used being adjusted to the gross amount of new equipment available. To maximize the growth rate, given the wage rate, is done in fig. 5.2, with α' the best technique given the wage rate w'. Then we apply the Samuelson Substitution Theorem and use this constant technique to expand output and employment at the highest possible rate over the very long period of transformation of the economy. Given the available stock of new equipment equal to $q_e (t-1)$ (fig. 5.4) the newly created sectors can operate at a rate $1+g$ and thus produce an enlarged output the following year which can again be operated at the same rate $1+g$, with consumption per head at c_t and total consumption C'_t and output at a rate $q_t = (1+g)q_{t-1}$, and so on indefinitely. This represents the greatest self-sustaining growth rate obtainable from the initial endowment of equipment (and perishables), and an inexhaustible labour supply. In the second year there will be the output of the new sector during year t plus the available surplus of equipment output from the old, pre-existing sectors, so that the amount of equipment available for the second year will be approximately double, so that the actually achieved growth will be $(1+g+s)$ where s is the contribution of existing sources which will gradually decline as the old sectors run down through non-replacement and as the new sectors rise through growth. Nothing is altered in the diagram since each year's output is again taken as unity, no matter how large.

Given the known spectrum of techniques, the wage rate determines the degree of intensity of equipment to choose and hence what variety of equipment to order. So long as the wage rate does not rise, there is no reason to change technique and hence no economic obsolescence. The importance of the skewness of α' by comparison with α becomes clear here. In the case of perishable goods only (fig. 4.15) there was very little difference between techniques for maximal growth and maximal consumption. But once the quantitative importance of durable equipment is admitted, growth has a strong affect of choice of technique (fig. 5.2) because the heavier the equipment, the smaller the growth rate which will exhaust the available surplus. To maximize g one wants light equipment, but light equipment means a low output and hence small surplus, so there is some point in between extremes which will give the maximum g.

Evidently the wage rate also enters basically into the maximal solution. In a capitalist or even a market economy, there is some wage that must be paid to industrial workers, even if there is heavy unemployment. This wage is commonly considerably higher than in the traditional crafts. The higher is this wage, the smaller the surplus and hence the lower the possible growth rate. This means choice of a more intensive type of equipment in order to get more output relative to the wages and consumption. A planned socialist community has a great advantage in that, in principle, it would accept as a fixed cost the consumption of the entire labour force whether employed or not. Therefore not only in social accounting but in practice the wage bill for the whole of the incremental output is nil. Therefore the maximum growth rate is the absolute maximum with zero wage rate. A much lighter equipment can be used with the result of a much higher growth rate. Even in a completely controlled and planned economy this extreme result would never be realizable—such things as on-site housing, higher consumption necessary for employed as opposed to unemployed labour, etc., would prevent it. Also some increase in wage rate would be necessary to obtain voluntary as opposed to forced mobility. Yet however the increased consumption is reckoned, it will certainly be lower than that considered by a private capitalist in a market economy, and hence will give rise to a higher growth rate. As shown in fig. 5.6, the effect of this maximal policy on incremental production is to shift the allocation of labour, production and equipment heavily towards the equipment industry. There is a longstanding confused and confusing argument for and against 'heavy' industry for rapid development. The

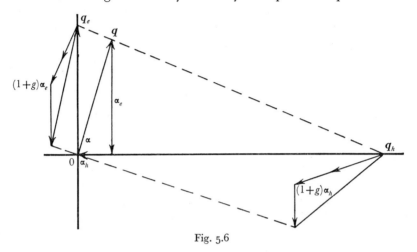

Fig. 5.6

implication of this analysis is the techniques employed should be 'light' but that the effort should be directed towards the equipment industries. Should these tend to 'heavier' than the perishable goods trades, the average technique will still not be very 'light'.

The effects on employment may be complex. There is commonly unemployment, employment in the traditional trades decreases: employment in the new sectors, though rising at a high rate, may be small, depending on how labour intensive the maximal growth rate is; finally the labour force usually is increasing. In any case it is highly likely, even with a 'light' technique, that the labour intensity of the new techniques is lower than that of the old, so that the reduction of employment in the one is not offset by the rise in the other initially. So that in the early stages there may be an acceleration of unemployment. However, compound growth rates are powerful levers and after a time the high growth rate in the new sector will first stop the growth in unemployment and then reduce it. Thus suppose after two or three years of putting all available resources into new industry, a country has 65 % of its employment in ancient industry, 5 % in newly equipped industry and 30 % unemployed. The labour force grows at 2 %, the run down of employment in ancient industry is at 5 % and the rate of growth of employment (and output) in the new industry is 10 %. After 5 years unemployment will have risen to 47 % and after 20 years to 59 %. However, between the years 20 and 30 employment in new industry begins to be massive and finally absorbs the falling employment in the old industry as well as the growth in the labour force. Then between 30 and 40 years, all the unemployment is absorbed into the new industries which are, by then, providing employment at a really rapid rate.

The strategy of such a programme is to devise a scheme for a high growth rate in industrial employment which will, as rapidly as possible, first absorb the unemployed and then overtake the natural increase. This cannot help but be a long process—thus the draining off of very low productivity labour in agriculture is not even yet completed in the U.K. or U.S.A. When and if it is accomplished, a heavy deceleration of growth rate is required. This means a rise in the share of output available for consumption. This change of pace makes possible techniques with much higher labour productivity, as an inspection of fig. 5.2 makes clear. When accomplished such a transformation will carry the economy as close as is possible, given the rate of growth of labour force, to the optimal consumption per capita. It does, however, require the total re-equipment with the more equipment-intensive types, and therefore, if it is to be accomplished by replacement of disappearing equipment, must be commenced well before the point of full employment is reached. Therefore a much more gradual deceleration and alteration of technique is indicated. Once the changeover is complete the populace can live by the Golden Rule in a Golden Age for ever after.

The strategy adopted is difficult to compare with other possible ones and hence it is difficult to demonstrate that it is indeed the most rapid method of industrialization. What it does do is give the greatest growth rate for the size of output, given the equipment available. But by choosing still less intensive equipment techniques, it may well be possible, by employing more labour, to have a larger product and hence surplus. Thus beginning with a higher output though a lower growth rate, one might be able to do better but it is unlikely. (*a*) If the same technique is kept, after a time, even though beginning higher, it will fall behind the smaller but faster growing model. (*b*) It is possible that with the larger accumulations of equipment, one could edge over to the maximum growth path, and arrive with a larger collection of equipment than the other method could manage. (*c*) But this is also objectionable because of durability—one is landed with the wrong type of low productivity equipment. The durability makes it important to choose the right kind of equipment from the start.

5.7. Accumulation in a market economy

The reasons for heavy unemployment in pre-capitalist economies remain somewhat obscure but they may well be due to special circumstances, such as the shortage of arable land which is here excluded by hypothesis. In so far as this model can help to explain, the argument would go somewhat as follows: there is a given semi-subsistence real wage; the wage determines the profit level and the appropriate best techniques. With this technique the scale of output and employment can be only so large as to require all the existing equipment. Then the existing stock of equipment determines employment (and unemployment). There seems no pressing tendency towards full employment. Presumably the wage is shared with varying degrees of equity between employed and unemployed (often the same person). If the degree of unemployment is too large leading to an intolerable average level of consumption, by the modern Malthusian argument (section 4.11), the work force may fall until a more tolerable level is reached. On the other hand in a fortunate community the unemployment level might be small, the resulting standard of living rather better than most, and the situation reasonably tolerable.

By contrast in developing economies the capitalist spirit tends to lead to accumulation out of profits. The low wage—high profits distribution has some justification if it leads to the accumulation of the equipment lack of which is impoverishing the community. The greater the proportion saved the greater is the justification, and also the nearer does the economy come to the optimal technique for the resulting rate of growth (section 4.8), though so long as the rates of profit and growth are unequal, the solution is sub-optimal. If the resulting rate of growth of output and employment is greater than the growth of the labour force, then average per capita consumption will be rising as unemployment decreases. As full employment is approached the rate of growth must decelerate. This could happen through the competitive bidding for labour in a tightening labour market—this would reduce profit rate and hence rate of saving and investment until growth rate equalled the natural increase. Should money wages rise but not real wages, there might still not fail to be a resolution—indeed there must be one, for continued accumulation with the same technique would lead to unemployed, redundant equipment. This could lead to a fall in the price of e and a lower profit rate in e, which, through a shift to h should lead to a generally lower profit rate. But at a lower profit a more intensive technique becomes profitable and this puts off, in part, the evil day of deceleration. Then added equipment is need both for capita and per capita growth.

These are boundary conditions, the contraints, if any, on the beginning and end of a trajectory. At one end is the level consumption and the quantity of equipment and at the other the rate of growth of labour force. The terminal constraint is of a special sort which casts its shadow long before, since it springs from coming up against the boundary condition of full employment. The economy begins with a low wage, growing output, unemployment continually supplemented by growing labour force and those thrown out of work by the decay of traditional industries under the impact of the newer technology. The effect of this is to give a long run to this state of the system with little or no tendency for wages to rise—even, on the contrary, they may fall as unemployment grows. Eventually, in most industrialized economies a general tightening of the labour market does occur, so that a deceleration of growth rate must follow. Unless this induces a reduction in capitalists' urge to accumulate out of profits, real wages must rise and profit rate fall. Then there ensures the long, slow deceleration because as the wage rate rises, more equipment-intensive methods become profitable which require accumulation at a greater rate than employment is growing. This postpones the required reduction in savings and profits. Gradually, by accumulating equipment per capita the economy arrives at the optimal point (fig. 5.2) where, given the labour force increase, any further accumulation of equipment per head leads to a fall in profit rate, and growth rate and which would lead to a renewed acceleration, which is ruled out by the labour force. So the economy has arrived at its boundary, satisfying its constraint, in a state which can persist indefinitely. But this smooth transition has been accomplished slowly because the full employment constraint is felt long before and yet its full impact can be postponed for so long by 'deepening'. It is as if a trans-Atlantic plane were to begin its run-in flight path for London in mid-Atlantic.

This transitional state is, in varying degrees, that of all the developed economies. Diagramatically it is difficult to exhibit because it involves a blending of a number of techniques as the economy creeps slowly up to higher and higher labour productivities with assorted equipment designed for the lower productivity techniques. Equipment is scrapped when it wears out or when it no longer yields enough after current materials inputs to cover the rising labour costs. When wages rise profits fall in current techniques and also net saving. The rate of profit on current techniques becomes less than on somewhat more productive ones. Hence all the expansion ('widening') of existing techniques ceases. Therefore all the output of e (gross) savings becomes available for fabrication in the newer techniques. Therefore two or more techniques will be operating simultaneously in each sector. The effect of this is that employment rises less than it would have had expansion of the old technique continued. The output destined for replacement furnishes less employment in its new form, as does the net increment to the stock of equipment, so that employment rises less, indeed it may even fall. With a slower growth of employment the pressure on the labour market eases and wages are less buoyant. However, profit rates are held up both by the moderation of wages and by the rise in productivity with the new technique, so that the deceleration of accumulation is also moderated.

By contrast with the case of perishables, the solution is not independent of the pattern of demand, because the consumers compete for the scarce supply of durables. If they were to demand a lower proportion of durables, more productive techniques could be employed yielding higher wages and greater real consumption of perishables. This fact of the importance of the pattern of demand leads straight into a much more serious problem. The rich have a different pattern from the poor, and in particular demand more durables, thus inhibiting output and growth. This raises sharply the issue of the rationale of profit. The function of profit is to guide producers to a choice of the best technique under the circumstances. But if it has, as a side effect, diversion of some of the profit into consumption and into consumption of goods that could raise overall productivity, then clearly profit is not leading to the optimal result. A socialist state, owning all productive equipment and receiving all profits, could distribute equally a part of these profits as a social dividend, with the result that actual demand would give a truer picture of the tastes of the community, and, in particular, lead to a lower demand for consumer durables and a higher productivity.

This is a clear example of a very important general point, easily overlooked, and yet casting doubt on a central proposition in economic analysis. The argument goes as follows: given demand, we find the optimal result by correct choice of technique and allocation of labour to achieve the fullest possible satisfaction of those wants. But the demands are not given: the demands effective in the market are conditioned and distorted by the productive process that is supposed to be satisfying them. If there is such a thing as demand, existing independently of a productive society—something very doubtful—then the actual demand as expressed in the market is not that demand but rather that demand filtered through the distributive effects of the productive effort to satisfy the actual demand. This is viciously circular. The analysis presented represents an attempt to avoid this emasculating circularity, but only, it must be admitted by assuming away a part of the problem, the inhomogeneity of the labour force.

5.8. Capitalist accumulation: malfunctioning

What can happen is not always what does happen and in this section we examine some of the ways in which *laissez-faire* capitalism can behave in a less functional way than that implied in section 5.7. Keynes suggested two related but distinct ways in which the system may function in a faulty fashion: the wage does not adjust so as to achieve full employment of labour; the existence of funds, and even of resources, for investment may not always result in actual investment. This perception has been strikingly broadened by the evidence that in pre-capitalist economies there is rarely if ever full employment.

The problem centres around investment, and hence inheres in the nature of the time structure of capitalist production, whereby present resources are the result of past activity, and the future, of present activity. The pricing-market mechanism is a remarkable instrument for signalling what actions are required in the present circumstances, but it gives little or no information about what actions (investment) are now desirable for future circumstances. Expectations about the future are of necessity mainly based on the present and recent past. What had largely escaped notice before Keynes was that the real possibility of perverse signalling by the market mechanism. Thus current activities are in part determined by investment, but if present activity is the basis of forecasting the future, then entrepreneurs are basing their actions on their actions, prophesies tend to be self-fulfilling. This circularity can be efficacious or pernicious—when times are good they are very good but when they are bad they are terrible.

The malfunctioning of the system is intimately bound up with Say's Law. If entrepreneurs invest little and hence produce little, by Say's Law, the demand for their goods is low, so that the self-fulfilling aspect is related to the neutral equilibrium by Say. On the other hand it is possible to break Say's Law, to move upwards or downwards from an equilibrium position. The issue arises in the model with the question of whether or not, when a portion of profits are saved, they will be invested, and, if invested, they will be matched by the necessary increased demand when the added equipment subsequently comes into operation. The problem goes back to the classical economists, much agitated Marx in the form of the Realization Problem and was revived by Sir Roy Harrod as a natural extension of the Keynesian analysis.

How inadequate Say is one can see in considering any growing system. If incomes equal value of output and are always and exactly re-spent for goods, then the aggregate values of net and gross national product will remain constant. But since real product is increasing prices must go down. The individual entrepreneur basing himself on current prices will suffer losses and may well at the very least, cease his investment in expansion. But if he does this, the value of aggregate demand will not remain constant but decline and this is almost certain to cause further contraction. Say is a very thin reed in such a storm.

To maintain even a constant price level in a growing state requires created credit each year in addition to the flow of savings out of income. This is concealed in the diagram because, each year, everything is returned to unit base, obscuring the fact that, at constant prices, last year's outlays no longer suffice. Therefore the flow of savings cannot satisfactorily regulate new investment. The problem is: what does determine the size and allocation of new investment each year. The market provides two kinds of information—price and cost, demand and output. Suppose that the wage, prices and most profitable techniques have been found, and that a large supply of unutilized labour exists. This means a single technique will be optimal over a considerable period. What the model shows is that there exists a steady state of growth, not that such a state ever has or will be realized.

Once profit rates have been equalized, price–cost relations give no help on the scale of production in each sector. The other signal given by the market is supply and demand. The individual producer may aim to produce what is demanded, but he cannot know in advance what will be demanded because for the totality it depends on what will be produced. The only information the market gives is last year's demand and this could be the simplest response of producers, but if it is, disaster ensues. The quantity demand will then be the wage bill, plus some fraction, say half, of last year's profits plus half last year's input demand, leaving unsold net output to the value of the remaining half of profits of last year. If profits were 20 %, demand will have gone down by 10 % the following year, and it will continue to fall indefinitely.

Although economists would never, until very recently, have told him to do so, the entrepreneur might look at last year's growth rate of demand as well as its level, and would be richly repaid for doing so—not the individual entrepreneur who might be sadly let down, but the totality of entrepreneurs. As we know there is one growth rate which would have exactly equated supply and demand so that if producers, observing supply equal to demand and the growth rate, continue with the same growth mode, they could plausibly remain in it, but the disturbing question is how could they ever get there in the first place? This is the stability question and can be asked as follows: if somehow the mechanism gets a bit out of step, will it return to the same path or depart further from it? The straightforward dynamic response pattern is that if demand is greater than supply, growth rate rises, and contrariwise if less than. Suppose there is a change in consumer expenditure pattern involving a shift of demand from h to e. Evidently such a mechanism is definitely unstable in aggregate even though it may be stable in its proportions. This is the opposite of Say's Law, relative output tending to be correct and aggregate outputs wrong. The point is that Say's Law is irrelevant since last year's output is being bought by this year's income, so the possible equality of the value of this year's output with this year's demand does not arise.

There is no question but that in fact no economy ever pursues an absolutely steady growth with neither shortages nor price changes. There are certain to be a variety of deviations from this straight and narrow path; the problem is to explain why such variations, in view of the inherent instability of the system, do not lead to complete collapse into inflation or total unemployment and starvation. From the evidence of the highly unsteady growth of capitalism, it is not really sound to look for explanations of stability which will restore the economy to its path of steady growth. Rather one should look for 'stability in the large' and 'instability in the small'. This means that the economy can never settle down to steady growth, but also that it also does not depart too far from its growth path, but rather hovers about it, being now above and now below it in a highly irregular position. Thus, although we are concerned with long run growth, the analysis required is a series of short run aberrations somehow related to the long run course.

5.9. An essay in the dynamics of long-run growth

The problem is to explain the broad outlines of long-run growth in the developed capitalist economies. This must be done without assuming a mechanism which automatically clears the labour market and yet it must explain why employment hovers somewhere in the neighbourhood of full employment—say 85 to 100 %. Also it should perform not locked in a steady state growth mode but grow irregularly with a pulse-like or alternating character.

The situation is as follows: inhibited solely by the quantity of equipment, the required real wage, and the consumption habits of rentiers, the economy has been growing in output and employment at a faster rate than the labour force. It has a low wage rate in relation to productivity and a low productivity in relation to known techniques. The low wage rate makes it unprofitable to adopt the higher productivity techniques but, at the same time it makes possible, a more rapid accumulation of the necessary equipment to realize the higher productivities. It is out of these opposing patterns that the model is constructed. There are thus two potential constraints on output—equipment and labour. But they differ in one fundamental respect—if it is profitable to do so, equipment can, given time, be increased to any extent whereas labour, though increasing, does so at a given rate.

Given the wage, investment at the existing profit rate increases the total rentier income and hence will be undertaken at the greatest rate possible given a supply of perishables, durables and labour. The economy has entered the general region of full employment of labour, which is no longer freely available. Increasingly entrepreneurs find it difficult to get the labour force that is necessary to man the new equipment, so they attempt to get labour from one another, and collectively, only succed in bidding up money wages.

The most difficult question is: does this or does it not result in higher real wages. If all producers maintain the same profit margins then the principal effect is inflation, but real wages are little effected. That this happens so completely as to cancel out the effect of the rise in money wages is doubtful. There are charges fixed in money terms so that producers do not need to raise prices proportionately to safeguard their profit rates. But most important of all is that since the labour is not so freely available, the rate of growth is bound to decline, which means, with the existing wage–profit relation, a deficient demand for goods. This leads either to accumulation of stock and/or to an actual further decrease in the growth rate which only makes the situation worse. In any case it is not a situation likely to support strong price increases.

If, then, real wages do rise, this changes the situation in favour of a higher productivity best technique. This shift which can only be gradual and only affect new equipment, means both that less resources are available for growth and that it takes more equipment to grow, both effects decelerate the growth rate.

It is possible for this process to proceed in a smooth way. As full employment is approached the real wage rate rises making a more equipment intensive technique the most profitable. Two effects follow: the rate of growth of equipment is reduced because the profit rate and the amount of equipment per head is greater, so the rate of growth of employment falls for two reasons, during the early stages of the transition. However, as an increasing share of output is produced by the higher productivity technique, the growth rate in employment can recover somewhat. The release of labour from the old techniques increases the effective labour force. When the changeover is complete, productivity is higher, wages are higher, profit and growth rates are lower, but not as much lower as they would have been with the old technique. If the growth rate in employment remains above that of labour force, the pressure on wages will reassert itself, a further fall in profit and growth rates will occur and a more intensive technique will be chosen. And so the process continues until growth rate in output and employment is equal to the growth rate of the labour force, at which point there is no more shortage of labour and steady growth with constant per capita income can go on for ever. Given the ratio of saving out of profits, this is optimal; wages and profit rates cannot both be higher. It is not absolutely optimal because if profit rate were to be reduced to the growth rate of output, employment and labour force, the very best technique would be chosen, one which would allow a higher per capita consumption than before.

The most important conclusion from this analysis is that the dynamic situation and properties determine a unique distribution of wealth—in sharp contrast to the static analysis where the distribution is arbitrary. Given the share of profits saved, there is only one wage rate which will produce the right amount of surplus available for that accumulation which will provide the goods and equipment to employ the increasing labour force.

As growth rate decelerates to labour force growth, the allocation of labour shifts to perishables because less net accumulation is required. Two effects counter-balance this shift. Higher productivities require more than proportional increases in equipment and hence in replacement and in gross output of equipment. Furthermore, the consumer competes with producers for durable goods. As income per capita rises, the proportions of consumer durables in the budget rises so raising the share of durables in output.

If there is no growth in the labour force the rate of profit must fall to zero, the wage must absorb the whole net product, output and employment cease to grow and consumption and net output are at the absolute maximum. Further accumulation would lead to higher gross output, but lower net output since the current inputs amount to more than the increase in net output.

Nothing is clearer than that capitalism does not progress in the smooth way suggested by this model, it goes by spurts and relapses. Exactly why and how it refuses to keep to the straight and narrow path is not so clear. However, a little closer inspection and more complete specification suggests that the model can also explain the irregular progress of capitalism. If, with a given technique, the economy grows too fast, wages go up and it grows more slowly; if it grows too slowly wages go down and it grows faster. All that is required is to show that when it grows too fast (too fast that is to be able to maintain its rate) it gets itself into a situation from which it will emerge growing too slowly. And when it grows too slowly it builds up a situation which will lead to too rapid a growth. Instead of sliding into a steady, maintainable growth, it bobs above and below it—which is exactly what capitalism from its earliest appearance has done.

Somewhat more complete specification of the behaviour of real wages is needed. This is given by the Phillips Curve, named after its discoverer Professor A. W. Phillips, who found that money wage rates rose or fell at a rate strongly influenced by the degree of unemployment. This agrees with the common experience that wage bargaining is most effective from the workers' point of view in a buoyant situation, and also with the fact that demands are always for an increase, not for a level of wages. To this must be added the proviso that price changes consequent on a wage change, in whichever direction, are always percentage-wise smaller than the wage change, so that money wages and real wages change in the same direction. These relations have been strikingly confirmed for the post-war period and are assumed to have held for earlier periods.

Capitalists are assumed to pursue profits under all circumstances. If a process is profitable, more of the same process will bring in more profits. Some proportion, taken to be constant only to simplify, of profits is saved. Accumulation goes forward at first only inhibited by existing supplies of raw materials and more particularly of equipment. As full employment of labour comes closer, real wages begin rising which is the form in which the labour force stock makes itself felt. As wages rise, the possible rate of growth declines. This may be for a time masked by inflation which mitigates the rise in real wages, but by permitting a persistence of the high growth rate of output and employment, it only brings on the acute stage of labour shortage the sooner, where, even with a constant real wage, the rate of growth would undergo deceleration.

As wages rise the growth rate of employment declines until it is equal to that of labour force. At this point unemployment has reached its lowest point and the rate of rise of real wages is at a maximum. As wages go higher, the rate of growth of employment falls below that of labour force and unemployment begins to grow again. But not until unemployment has reached a considerable proportion will the wage rate cease rising and reach its maximum. This is then the lowest point of the growth rate of employment and hence the point of maximum growth of unemployment. With large unemployment wages begin to fall and growth rate to rise again. So long as the growth of employment is lower than that of labour force, unemployment continues to rise with the fall in wage rates accelerating. When at last growth has accelerated back to equality with labour force growth unemployment grows no more and is at its maximum, as is the rate of decline of real wages. This means that employment proceeds to grow faster than labour force, and keeps on rising until it has reduced unemployment to the point of zero wage change. But, since employment is growing faster than supply, unemployment must keep on decreasing and so pushes wages slowly up and employment growth down, and so on through another cycle.

Thus employment is geared to the labour force without assuming it to be so. Furthermore, the mechanism to accomplish this generates an economic behaviour that is in accord with reality. There are shifts in the distribution of income between wages and profits over the cycle but the average from cycle to cycle is constant. Profit rate varies over the cycle but is constant in the long run. Most important of all, this mechanism requires almost no quantitative assumptions, it operates by virtue of its structure alone.

Now complicate the model by allowing for choice of techniques. As full employment is approached the rise of wages and the fall in the profit rate starts a process of shifting to a more intensive technology, but the wage rise continues although the shift is only getting underway. Secondly, because of the greater equipment intensity, the same rate of flow of funds and resources results in a smaller amount of employment than would have the same amount with the old technique. Therefore labour is 'released', i.e. there is technological unemployment to add to the already existing unemployment, so that the pressure on the labour market is lessened as is the tendency if wages rise. The most important thing is that wages can rise higher with the new techniques than with the old before they seriously lessen the rate of accumulation. With a single technique the rate of profit is sharply reduced by a rise in real wage rates but with more productive technique available the impact of a rise in wages can be moderated by a shift to the use of more equipment per worker. Thus the shift in technique increases the available labour force and lessens the demand for labour from any rate of accumulation. The result is that the expansion can continue longer, but, as the transition is completed and the same rate of growth is continued, the pressure arises again and the wage starts to rise again. Although postponed, the contradiction emerges in that, with growth rate reduced to natural increase, unemployment is at its minimum, wages are rising at their maximum rate and the equality of growth rates of employment and labour force cannot be maintained. Unemployment increases again and wages either fail to rise much or actually fall, in spite of the higher level of productivity. But to restore the high growth level wages do not have to return to their previous level.

This model of irregular capitalist growth is much too simple to give an adequate description of the actual historical process. But as a broad outline it has almost all the requisite characteristics. It is essential in analysing capitalism to escape from the preoccupation with steady growth rates: these are very helpful in grasping the general situation and possibilities but do not even approach reality. This can be seen easily if one imagines, as is certainly the case, that growth is often too weak to maintain full employment. If later, the economy does reach reach full employment, then it must have grown at a pace that cannot be maintained, and the resulting deceleration is almost certain to overshoot and lead again to too slow a pace. Yet the economy does stay near full employment and does tend to return to it from time to time. This seems intimately connected with the fact that, wages rates do rise over time and that profit rates do not. In the early phases of capitalism, dominated by technological unemployment, wage rates do not tend to rise. But in the later phases, when accumulation has long continued and when high productivity makes it fairly easy, this accumulation presses on labour supply and pushes up real wages. If there is a fairly steady growth rate of labour force and if, on the average, employment does tend to grow at this rate, then accumulation will on the average form a constant fraction of output. If profits are the principal source of this accumulation, and if a fairly constant proportion of profits are accumulated, then it follows that profits are, on the average, a fairly constant proportion of output. By the same token, so are wages. Therefore we get roughly constant distribution shares, a well-substantiated fact. But whereas the constant share of wages consists of a falling labour/output ratio and a rising wage rate, profits consist of a constant π and capital/output ratio. At this point the model is unsatisfactory, for the profit rate is falling (it must fall to force the rise in productivity). To this point, along with others, the next section is devoted.

5.10. Technical progress

A change for the better in the known spectrum of techniques is called technical progress. Normally it consists of a new technique with one or more smaller input coefficients. Throughout most of history these discoveries have arisen out of the whole fabric of social and cultural life in some complex way which, to the economist, must simply be taken as given. In recent years it has been found that improvements can sometimes be produced to order by spending money on research and development. This brings progress, in part at least, within the framework of economic analysis instead of leaving it as a datum, but this line of thought will be ignored here.

These improvements are usually highly specific to one or a few industries but in a semi-aggregation model like this the behaviour is the result of thousands disparate and more or less independent discoveries. It is therefore sometimes appropriate to consider a steady reduction of input coefficients. An improvement may be the alteration of the coefficients of an existing process or be an entirely new one. It may affect one process only, or many, or conceivably, all. The most important thing to keep in mind is that whatever form it takes, it will rarely, if ever, alter the input coefficients of already installed 'fixed' equipment, which has been built from the previously used technique. Therefore gross investment is required to realize the input reductions and it will take time, sometimes considerable time, before they can be fully realized.

The improvements may take the form of reducing the inputs of perishables, e.g. greater efficiency in burning fuels, or of equipment, or of labour. Again, it may mean the use of more equipment, but yielding a greater output per capita than was possible before. And, of course, it makes all the difference which of these predominates.

There is a constrast between the situation of underdeveloped economies and the more developed ones. The former have already available a great range of more productive techniques which are known but not usable for lack of equipment (as well as skills and social forms) whereas the developed economies can only evolve a greater productivity by lower profit rates. In the course of the development of the capitalist countries these techniques were not known and as they were gradually developed they were exploited. This process did not necessarily involve the reduction of the rate of profit; they were exploited as they became operational. In fact capitalist economic development has shown little if any evidence of the falling rate of profit. More equipment and higher productivity has been prompted not by higher wage rates and lower profit rates but rather by technical innovations. As an example, in fig. 5.7, α_1' represents such a discovery; it requires more equipment but increases labour productivity more than enough to compensate. At the previous price p_0, α_1 would earn a higher profit rate, be able to pay a higher wage and in either case be able to expand relatively to the other sector. After a long period of transition

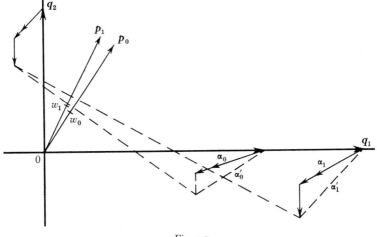

Fig. 5.7

with p_0 changing to p_1, a higher wage, w_1, can be paid, both by sector h and sector e. This shows how the fruits of technical progress are disseminated in the economy. A continual stream of such innovations would tend to have a broadly similar effect on both sectors. Therefore technical progress may be visualized as a gradual shifting outward of both α's, with possibly a moderate tendency for the slope and length to increase.

In these circumstances suppose the wage rate were to remain constant; the profits rate would increase, and so, with a constant per cent saved and invested, the growth rate would steadily accelerate, leading, eventually, to a serious shortage of labour. Wages would rise and decelerate growth; but also they would rise higher and lead to a renewed growth in unemployment. Thus rates overshoot; the unemployment would induce a decline, or perhaps only a stagnation; whilst profit and growth rates would again rise and so on. The basic alteration in the mechanism here is that a falling rate of profit is not necessary (nor is it ruled out).

With a perfect adjustment, the growth could proceed in a steady state as follows: the level of wages should be such that the rate of profit is such that, given the fraction of profits unconsumed, the growth rate can be such as to equip the added workers plus those released from failure to replace old equipment. In addition there must be just that amount of unemployment which ensures that wage rates rise at the rate of growth of labour productivity. Such a steady state can persist indefinitely, but, of course, it does not: all manner of things will throw one or more of these conditions out and then the irregular growth reappears. Thus suppose the unemployment rate is increased by a temporary flow of immigration; this means wages rise less or even not at all. The result is profit rate rises, entrepreneurs can accelerate growth without running into inflation. This growth rate, higher than the continuing growth in labour force, brings eventually a return to a rise in wages equal to that of productivity, but the growth rate in employment being higher leads to a further fall in the percentage of unemployment and to wage rates rising faster than productivity. This may lead to inflation, but it must necessarily lead to a deceleration in growth rate. The deceleration in growth rate leads to a growth in the percentage unemployment a pushing back of wage growth to that of productivity. This position cannot be held because, now employment is growing less rapidly than labour force, unemployment grows and wages fall behind productivity, thus restoring profitability and the surplus which will permit of a resumption of rapid expansion. Since productivity is always rising, the phase of rising wages and rapid growth will tend to be larger than the depressed phase in which wages fall and productivity rises, thus rapidly generating a suitable gap.

In this way the basic features of capitalist growth can be explained—wages rates rise and profit rates remain about the same. In the early stage, with limited employment, supplemented by technological unemployment, there is the grim phase of high growth rate with low wages which tend to remain there. In the later stages real wages show a definite secular upward tendency and just as surely profits show none. The remarakble fact is that these quite diverse behaviours produce the result of roughly constant relative shares.

Since the saving rate is assumed to be an institutionally determined constant proportion of profit rate, the behaviour of accumulation as a share of net output is the same as that of profits. Therefore if profits are to form a constant share of output, technical progress must leave the productivity of equipment unchanged whilst raising that of labour.

6

ESSAYS IN APPLIED ECONOMICS:
INPUT–OUTPUT

The aim of this chapter is to indicate a few of the directions in which the model may be developed in order to bring it closer to reality and to permit of a somewhat richer variety of results. The reader should be able, within this general framework to do the detailing in whatever direction his interests lie. Obvious directions in which to develop the analysis are economic planning, fiscal policy, wage and price policy, international trade and the balance of payments and cybernetic stabilizers, but there are, of course, many more.

6.1. The checkerboard scheme

To bring out the basic fact that every purchase is a sale, the transactions of any economy can be recorded in rows and columns, one for each product. The rows represent allocation of output, the columns the inputs by source; there may be as many rows and columns as is convenient or practicable. The striking fact is that the data required to fill in the squares of the checkerboard are simple and in principle easily available, though in practice, it is a skilled and laborious task. The data are usually in monetary form; dividing by appropriate price gives output and demand structure; dividing by quantities yields price and costs structure. Finally, the checkerboard of coefficients, known as a Leontief Matrix after its originator, is derived from the division of each input by the relevant output. It is at this point that the connection is made between fact and the theory that has been sketched out in this book. It must be admitted that the assumptions made in the theory do no coincide completely or even satisfactorily with the conditions under which the data rise. Yet the great importance of this conjunction of theory and of fact cannot possibly be overstressed. However interesting a theory may be it is of no use unless it can be verified or falsified in a sense which makes it applicable to a wide range of cases. The house of economics is filled with a great collection of pretty toys that can never be taken down and put to use. Cruder, more awkward tools like input–output analysis are by, their extraordinary simplicity, actually usable and hence desirable.

Economists tend to exaggerate the amount of flexibility and substitutability in production. No doubt there is known a vast range of methods of production but once a choice has been made and production undertaken, the flexibility is severely circum-scribed. There is some choice of processes in specifying new equip-ment but production is necessarily done with existing equipment according to existing procedures in a fixed and almost unalterable way. In the long run these processes gradually alter but even with these, where the Samuelson Substitution Theorem is applicable, there is no change. In this chapter we undertake a more intensive analysis of behaviour with fixed techniques of production. The extension of the analysis to any number of sectors is obvious and in principle straightforward, but it cannot be accomplished graphically.

Output theory shows how levels of net demand, e.g. consump-tion and investment determine the scale of output, its general level, and the proportions, i.e. its distribution among the sectors. The two together fix the volume of employment. The theory of price, its dual, describes how scale, the price level, and proportion, rela-tive prices, result from the common wage and profit ratios, and how out of the whole arises the resulting distribution of income. These twins provide the minimal necessary skeleton analytic structure upon which more specific and detailed assumptions may be grafted to elucidate particular problems. By virtue of the linearity assumption the twins may be studied separately as well as together.

6.2. Output and employment multipliers

All demand for goods may be divided into that derived from inputs and the rest, often called the final bill of goods. These latter goods are net output—the output left after subtraction of the output needed as input in producing. Commonly it is divided into consumption, investment, government expenditure and exports, but further complication are possible and sometimes desirable. Each must be specified as to its structure, i.e. the amount demanded from each sector, but they can all be simply added to a single vector, u, of net output demanded, since it does not matter who is demanding so long as good demanded is homogeneous.

There are various ways of approaching the analysis of the effects of given net demands. First, to see the nature of the problem, consider what is the result of a set of demands which first arise in some period and remain constant at that level indefinitely. Assume that entrepreneurs have adequate stocks of goods and that they set level of production in period $t + 1$ equal to the amount demanded in t. If the economy was previously in equilibrium, output can be measured in deviations from the equilibrium values, which amounts to taking the previous level as zero and studying only the increments resulting from the new increase in net demand.

In the initial period output remains zero, but sales equal $\bar{u}_0$. Then in $t = 1$, output is put at $q_1 = \bar{u}_0$ and this output leads to a demand for input so that sales rise by this amount. Output is again raised in $t = 2$ with a consequent further rise in sales and so on. The question is: will this process go on or does it level off and if it does level off, by how much will the gross output rise by comparison with the rise in net demands? To deal with the problem in full generality it is useful to ask two separate questions: what will be the effect of a unit rise in the demand for good one alone, and, separately, for good two? Once found, the gross output required for unit net output of each good, the output required for 5 units or 50 million units net will be 5 or 50 million times that for one unit. Similarly, the effect for a drop of 1 unit is found by simply reversing the signs. Thus from these two results we get the result for any change whatsoever in level of net demand. Instead of adding each period's demand for input to the given net demand, it is more convenient to formulate the same thing in another way: the change in output is made equal to the current difference between the given net demand and the current net output (current gross output less input). Thus producers are, throughout the process, setting output equal to demand but are always, inevitably failing to achieve the equality because of the consequent effects of their effort to do so on the demand for their own and for others products.

Starting from a unit rise in the given demand, $\bar{u}_1$, for good one, the first few sequential stages are given in fig. 6.1. The initial output is at the origin; output in the first period is at $q_1 = +1$ on the horizontal axis, with net output at u_1 and the rise in output to the next period is the difference between q_1 and u. This leads to q_2 with an increase in both outputs. The inputs are found by increasing everything in proportion; subtracting them

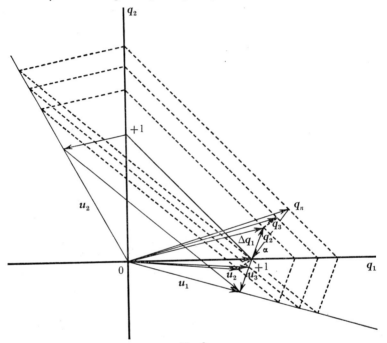

Fig. 6.1

from q_2 gives u_2. So long as u is less than $\bar{u}$, q increases, but an increase in q brings an increase in u, so if u is below $\bar{u}$, u increases towards $\bar{u}$, and the opposite if u is greater than $\bar{u}$. Likewise if u lies to the left of $\bar{u}$, then q moves to the right, as does u. Similarly, if u lies to the right of $\bar{u}$, then q and u hence move leftwards towards $\bar{u}$. Thus we see that the process converges necessarily to an equilibrium q_n with a net output equal to $\bar{u}$, so that no further change ensures. The output once determined when applied to the labour input coefficients, gives the employment, both by sector and the total. The path to equilibrium may include oscillations in the proportions but the magnitude of q never ceases growing.

It is evident that it is the viability of any existing economy which insures stabliity of the process by making the locus of u rise with increasing gross output.

Since to exist any economy must be viable, all such multiplier processes gradually die away and a finite, stationary equilibrium multiplier necessarily exists. By inspection of the graph it is evident that the less viable the economy (the nearer the two u's come to forming a $180°$ angle) (a) the slower will be the process proceed and (b) the larger are the multipliers. This is because the flatter the angle, the less will a given increase in q raise the locus of u. Therefore degree of stability and size of multipliers are directly related. It is a question of relation of net to gross product; if to increase net product by some amount, the gross product has to be greatly increased, then the economy is less stable and, by the same token the multipliers are large.

There are, for two goods, 4 multipliers (n^2 for n goods) as shown in fig. 6.2. The multipliers being ratios, are independent of scale and hence there is no necessity to take a unit fixed, net demand. The multiplier for net good one to gross good one is oc/ob and for one two is cd/ob, that for two to one is fg/oe and two to two of/oe. Suppose these were respectively $1·20$, $0·20$, $0·90$ and $1·33$, it is convenient to arrange them in tabular form:

$$\begin{Bmatrix} Q_1 \\ Q_2 \end{Bmatrix} = \begin{Bmatrix} 1·20 \\ 0·20 \end{Bmatrix} \bar{U}_1 + \begin{Bmatrix} 0·90 \\ 1·33 \end{Bmatrix} \bar{U}_2.$$

These are the constituent multipliers which hold regardless of the size of the components of $\bar{u}$, for the whole of any given, net demands as well as increments. Thus if $\bar{U}_1$ is 75 and $\bar{U}_2$ is 150, the result is

$$Q_1 = 90 + 144 = 234,$$
$$Q_2 = 15 + 213 = 228.$$

For any particular $\bar{u}$ there is only a pair of multipliers but these multipliers are different for every different $\bar{u}$, unlike the four constituent multipliers.

It is important to note that these are equilibrium values and hence never actually observed; they are the values which would be approached if the given demand never changed. But it does change, yet this does not invalidate the analysis, it only requires a slight modification. We may dissect the dynamical behaviour of an economy by applying to it either a step function as above or an impulse function and it is this latter that is more useful for a changing level of given demands. Given a unit demand for good one in the first period, with nothing before and nothing after,

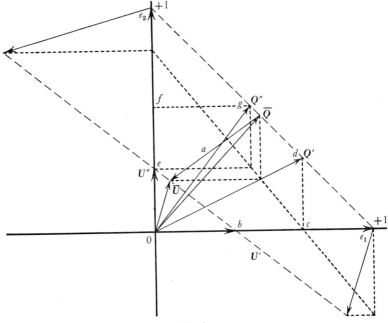

Fig. 6.2

what happens? In the next period output of good one is unity and this gives rise to the corresponding demands (small) for inputs; hence in the next period arise outputs equal to these inputs and so on. Similarly for good two. For each good a demand for X units gives rise to subsequent effects exactly X times as large at each point as those for unit demand. Therefore we have only to work out once and for all the effects of a unit impulse on each sector and we then find out by massive and careful calculation what is the actual behaviour of the economy for any time series of given net demands. Measuring in deviations from equilibrium, the impulses may be negative as well as positive. Each impulse gives rise to a successive pattern of input demands which decays according to a set pattern. Thus in period 4, for a system that was in equilibrium, we have the new given demand, plus that of period 3 once decayed, and that of period two twice decayed plus that of the first period thrice decayed. Suppose a productive structure given by

$$\begin{matrix} \text{I} & 0\cdot15 & 0\cdot60, \\ 2 & 0\cdot20 & 0\cdot25. \end{matrix}$$

Unit demand from last period gives rise to demand now of

$$\begin{matrix} \text{I} \\ 2 \end{matrix} \begin{Bmatrix} 0\cdot15 \\ 0\cdot20 \end{Bmatrix} \text{I} + \begin{Bmatrix} 0\cdot60 \\ 0\cdot25 \end{Bmatrix} \text{I} = \begin{Bmatrix} 0\cdot75 \\ 0\cdot45 \end{Bmatrix}.$$

Unit demands two periods ago gave rise to this demand last period so that now the demand is

$$\begin{matrix} \text{I} \\ 2 \end{matrix} \begin{Bmatrix} 0\cdot15 \\ 0\cdot20 \end{Bmatrix} 0\cdot75 + \begin{Bmatrix} 0\cdot60 \\ 0\cdot25 \end{Bmatrix} 0\cdot45 = \begin{Bmatrix} 0\cdot12 \\ 0\cdot15 \end{Bmatrix} + \begin{Bmatrix} 0\cdot27 \\ 0\cdot11 \end{Bmatrix} = \begin{Bmatrix} 0\cdot39 \\ 0\cdot26 \end{Bmatrix}.$$

And unit demands three periods ago gave rise to this demand last period, so that they now result in

$$\begin{matrix} \text{I} \\ 2 \end{matrix} \begin{Bmatrix} 0\cdot15 \\ 0\cdot20 \end{Bmatrix} 0\cdot39 + \begin{Bmatrix} 0\cdot60 \\ 0\cdot25 \end{Bmatrix} 0\cdot26 = \begin{Bmatrix} 0\cdot06 \\ 0\cdot08 \end{Bmatrix} + \begin{Bmatrix} 0\cdot16 \\ 0\cdot07 \end{Bmatrix} = \begin{Bmatrix} 0\cdot22 \\ 0\cdot15 \end{Bmatrix}.$$

The process can be followed backwards until the present results become negligible, or until the economy was in equilibrium. These numbers are called a weighting function because they apply the appropriate reduced weights to past demands. Thus suppose the economy were in equilibrium up to 3 periods ago and thereafter experiences the following time series of given net demands:

$$\begin{matrix} & t-3 & t-2 & t-1 & t \\ \text{I} & 35 & 14 & 1 & 8 \\ 2 & 10 & 2 & -5 & -4 \end{matrix}$$

Demand at time t will be made up as follows:

$$\begin{matrix} \text{I} \\ 2 \end{matrix} \begin{Bmatrix} 8 \\ -4 \end{Bmatrix} + \begin{Bmatrix} 0\cdot15 \\ 0\cdot20 \end{Bmatrix} \text{I} + \begin{Bmatrix} 0\cdot60 \\ 0\cdot25 \end{Bmatrix} (-5)$$

$$+ \begin{Bmatrix} 0\cdot12 \\ 0\cdot15 \end{Bmatrix} 14 + \begin{Bmatrix} 0\cdot27 \\ 0\cdot11 \end{Bmatrix} 2 + \begin{Bmatrix} 0\cdot06 \\ 0\cdot08 \end{Bmatrix} 35 + \begin{Bmatrix} 0\cdot16 \\ 0\cdot07 \end{Bmatrix} 10$$

which adds to outputs (in deviation from equilibrium) of

$$\begin{matrix} \text{I} & 11\cdot07, \\ 2 & 0\cdot14. \end{matrix}$$

No multiplier is observable but it is all the result of constant structural multipliers.

Whilst it is logically admissible to take net demands as given and study their effects on output, it is at best a partial explanation if the level and rate of change of output have direct or indirect effects on the net demands. Certainly consumption alters as, less certainly, does investment, and, progressively less certainly, government demand and exports. There problems are treated briefly below in section 6·8.

6.3. Prices set by wages and profits

As gross output must be large enough and properly proportioned to produce a net product equal to given demands, so prices must be high enough and in the right proportions to yield a surplus sufficient to cover wages and profit. But here the parallel ends; the manner of functioning is quite different in the twin systems. Relative and absolute prices are not determined simply by generating enough operating profit to cover wages and profits, but they must be such as to yield equal wage and profit rates in widely different productive structures. Suppose a fixed pair of techniques for producing perishable goods only with everything measured in per capita terms. In the long run equilibrium wage and profit rates must be equal and materials cost plus wage cost plus profits must exhaust the value of the product.

Given a profit rate, relative prices and the real wage rate are uniquely determined but not the money wage rate or the price level. A price ray normal to the line connecting alpha $(1+\pi)\alpha_1$, with $(1+\pi)\alpha_2$ will give equal value of product less input cost with profits, i.e. the projections of u_1' and u_2' in fig. 6.3. Each sector therefore has the same amount to disburse, per worker, for wages with profits, i.e. $(1+\pi)w$. If the price level, whatever it is, is taken as unity (unit length of P), then the money wage must be the same fraction of unity that ow is of the length of p, say 0·25, or put the other way round, if the wage is 10 the price level is 40. It is not necessary, only convenient, to work with unit price level. Where the price level is arbitrary, the value of u_1' and u_2' is their projection on P multiplied by its length. If in the diagram the money wage is w_1' twice that of w, the price vector p' will be twice the length but same slope as p and the value of u' for any output, will also be twice as large and equal to $(1+\pi)w'$. Therefore, with given profit rate, altering the money wage alters the price level but leaves the real wage and relative prices unaffected.

A given profit rate determines the real wage and substantially, but not quite completely, the distribution of income. Wages constitute a different proportion of the value of the various goods and

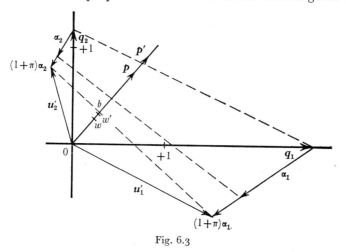

Fig. 6.3

hence a given real wage will be a different share of product depending on the composition of output. For unchanged relative outputs a given profit rate will determine both the real wage and the distribution of income. What it does do is to determine the share of profits in gross product independently of output. For each good $(1+\pi)$ cost = value of product, but profits are a fraction, π, of cost so the share of profits for each good and for all goods together is $\pi/1+\pi$.

The functioning of the economy determines, in some complex way, the money wage rate and the profit rate, which though a pure number can also be considered a money profit rate since it is a ratio of two money quantities. Then the price level turns these two into real quantities. Though the profit rate determines the real wage, the money wage rate does not determine the profit rate. What it does do is fix a relation between prices and profit rate, the selection of any pair of which will then determine real wages as well.

To see this consider fig. 6.4 where there is a given range of per capita real net product, $q - \alpha = u$, to dispose of. There is a given money wage, w; also there is a unit reference price level p. If the price level is low enough we can have a uniform profit level of zero with a price ray normal to the locus of u and a price

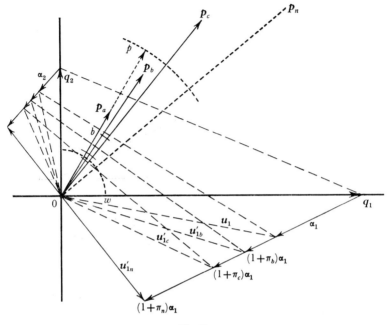

Fig. 6.4

level given by P_n whose length is the same fraction of that of p that ow is of ob. ob is the projection of u on p_n and its value is reduced, by the length of P_a, to ow. A higher profit rate b generates a lower locus of u'_b; the equilibrium price ray determines a different set of relative prices but also requires higher price level P_b to raise the projection on it of u'_b to the level of $(1 + \pi_b)w$. Thus the real wage is lowered but by a somewhat indefinite amount since relative prices have altered. A still higher profit rate, π_c, determines new relative prices and requires a price level, P_c, greater than unity to raise the value of $U'_c \cdot P_c$ to $(1 + \pi_c)w$, thus reducing further the real wage. As the price level is increased without limit, the real wage declines towards zero; π approaches its limiting maximum value π_n and the price ratio goes to its limiting value given by the ray P_n.

These results only follow if prices are cost determined. If prices are sticky in both upward and downward directions, then the direct, reverse relation of Ch. 4 exists. A rise in money and real wages means a fall in profit rate and an alteration in relative prices. A rise in the profit rate must mean a fall in money and real wages.

6.4. The wage–price inflationary process

There are good grounds, both empirical and analytical, for holding that rate of profit tends to remain unchanged. This gives a simple and lucid explanation of the inflationary process. It is convenient to revert to ordinary rather than per capita quantities. This requires use of the labour input vector a_l giving the quantity of labour per unit of output. Money cost per unit of output is than wa_l. Fully competitive markets have continuous price formation but are not describable by mark-up theory. Most prices are administered prices, which means they have, at intervals, to be set. These intervals vary widely and do not coincide but not much realism is lost and a great deal of simplicity gained by assuming that there is one standard period, at the end of which all sectors state a price for the forthcoming period based on their costs for the period ending.

Although essential the cause is not completely agreed, the nature of the inflationary process has become clearer in industrialized, fully employed nations. One man's price is another man's cost. A rise in prices is a rise in costs and a rise in costs leads to a rise in prices and so on *ad infinitum*. The question is whether such a process is self-sustaining or whether it peters out. If the latter, what starts off such a process and what may keep renewing it?

A uniform rise in wages leads, in varying degrees, according to labour intensity, to rises in cost. Next period prices are raised to cover the higher costs. But this in turn leads to higher costs reapportioned in a complicated way determined by the cost structure of the various sectors. Suppose the economy to be originally in equilibrium and call these prices and wages zero. There is a fixed profit mark-up rate π giving a fixed net product, u', for paying wages with interest. At time zero the wage rate rises from zero to a constant $\bar{w}$, leading to higher constant wage costs of $(1 + \pi)wa_l = \bar{v}'$ and to losses, during period zero, of this amount since prices had been set on the basis of a zero wage rate. Thus in period a, prices are raised by enough to cover increased cost, including mark-up (fig. 6.5), so that $\bar{v}' = \Delta p = P_a$. In period a the wage cost remains v' and the amount available for wages X'_a is value of product less materials cost, the components of X' being $u'_1 \cdot P_a$ and $u'_2 \cdot P_a$. Since both u's have less than unit length, the length of X'_a is bound to be less than that of v' so that there is a general loss, counting normal profit as a cost. In the example industry 2 has high labour cost and raised price much more than 1 with the result that the increase in p_1 does not even cover increased materials cost, apart from the new labour cost. Prices are then raised at the end of period a by enough to cover the added costs both labour and material, as of the prices ruling in period a, so that $X'_a + \Delta p_a = \bar{v}'$. In period b these higher prices mean unforeseen increases in costs so that the goal of covering costs is still not achieved. X'_b will be no longer, since all prices have risen, and will alter direction depending on where the greater losses are. X'_b has grown towards the fixed $\bar{v}'$ and has altered its direction towards it: therefore the third round of price changes, both level and proportions, will be smaller. That X' will gradually approach $\bar{v}'$, and hence bring the price changes to an end, can be seen as follows: X' is shorter than p because the u''s are less than unity; whenever p shifts X' shifts in the same direction but by a smaller amount; since $\bar{v}' - X'$ determines the shifts in p, it also determines those in X' and it does so in such a way as always to diminish the discrepancy between the two; therefore X' tends towards $\bar{v}'$ and p tends to an equilibrium p_n; the system is dynamically stable.

Since $\bar{v}'$ is positive, X' must also be, therefore both projections must be positive and hence p must lie within the angle formed by the oz_1 and oz_2, the normals to u'_1 and u'_2. The less viable the economy, the narrower is this angle and more importantly, the smaller are the projections of the u''s on any p. Then to raise X' to v', the greater must be the length of P and hence the lower the real wage. This means a slower approach to equilibrium, so that the degree of viability determines how stable the system is.

This result applies not only to an increment in wages but also to a decrement and to the equilibrium level of wages and of prices as

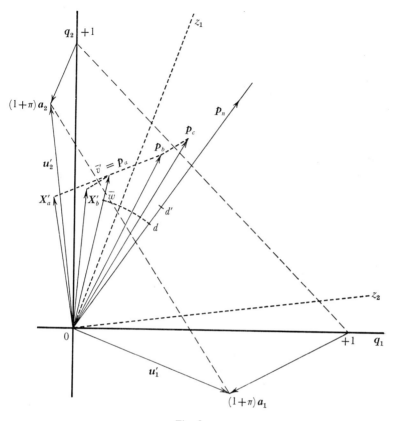

Fig. 6.5

well. Hence, given the profit and wage rates, the absolute and relative prices are determined. In the equilibrium value, if wages are doubled, $\bar{v}'$ is also, so that w determines the price level but not relative prices in agreement with the earlier conclusions.

Given π, the real wage is determined, or given the real wage, π is determined. But suppose both are determined independently, what then happens? It is then an over-determined system and will normally lead to inconsistant results which cannot be realized in practice. Such incompatibles can be resolved dynamically. Suppose that, for whatever reason, capitalist producers maintain a firm, constant profit mark-up and that by altering price they are always able to enforce it ex ante at least. Because of relatively full employment of labour, workers bargain for a high real wage and producers, however must they protest, are fairly ready to grant the wage demand because they have the escape offered by a higher future price.

Given P_n and the wage w in fig. 6.5 the real wage may be measured by od/oP_n. The workers obtain a money wage of od'; this leads to a price rise by the amount of the increased wage cost the next period and subsequently smaller and smaller increases until a new price level is reached higher in the same proportion as the increased wage. By this time the workers have lost their initial gain and capitalists have regained their initially reduced, ex post, profit margins. Since the real situation is a tightness in the labour market, the workers should, and in fact do, react by raising their money wage to bring it back to their real wage demand of od'/oP. Realism suggests more frequent price changes than wage changes, which slows up the process, but for simplicity assume wages, like prices are renegotiated each perod.

When prices in the second period rise, wages are raised a second time, so that in the third period prices will be having a compound rise—the initial rise doubled now, plus a further rise due to the previous period's rise in input prices. Wages will again be raised and this time by a larger amount. As the process continues both prices and wages will tend towards a state of constant proportional growth. Neither workers nor capitalists get what they aim for, but workers have succeeded in raising real wages, and capitalists are forced to accept a fall in the realized rate of profit. There is a double fall in the rate; the ex post rate is lower than planned and the real rate is below the money rate because of rising prices. Of course, it is likely that producers will begin to anticipate price rises by changing to a higher ex ante mark-up; likewise the money rate will tend to rise in an attempt to restore the real rate. Both of these would accelerate the price rise and in turn lead to further behavioural changes. Furthermore, relative prices will be distorted by the process. The initial response of p is in the direction of P_a not the final and equilibrium direction of P_n. The second change is still mostly in the direction of P_a and only gradually does it alter course towards P_n. Meantime each new rise in wages pushes prices off course again, so that, eventually, there will be an assortment of compounded effects, one each of P_a, P_b, P_c, ..., etc.; to P_n. Technical progress in the form of a shortening of either a_1,

a_2, or a_t makes possible smaller price rises and greater ones in real wages.

This melancholy process has been one of the notable features of the post-war economic climate. Its cause and its cure are fogged by the phenomenon of 'leap frogging'. A disaggregated model is necessary for its analysis, which can easily be carried out with a diagram like that of fig. 6.5. The workers in industry 1 get a rise in wage rate which leads to an initial price rise in 1. This then leads to subsequent price rises in both 1 and 2, which leads the workers in 2 to claim not necessarily a rise in real wages but a rise in money wages, to compensate for the price rise. Their claim is bound to be influenced by the level of the money wage in 1. A second rise will set off a second train of price rises which still stimulate further wage claims first in 1 and than again in 2. The basic issue here, the redistribution of income between profits and wages, is almost totally obscured by a quite different issue, the redistribution of wages between sectors. Adding technical progress makes the true complexity appear. A wage claim may then not be for a redistribution of income or wages, but merely for a restoration of the status quo ante in respect of income generated within the sector. But this is bound to affect other wage earners and profit takers, and, of course, a claim may really be for a redistribution of income and hence a challenge to the existing social order. It may also be a claim for the present generation against the future generations, if net accumulation is largely done out of profits.

6.5. Cycle generation by stocks-output reaction

In section 6.2 output and employment are pictured as moving steadily towards their equilibrium values—something that does not happen in reality. To see why, we note that at each step demand is greater than output, indeed it is this discrepancy that produces the resolution. The consequence is that there is an accumulated decline in the stocks of finished goods, whether held by producers, middlemen or retailers. A continued decline in stock, however mild, cannot be ignored. Production must be expanded not only because of larger demand but also for restocking.

Assume that producers desire to keep a given level of stocks and that initially they have this level. If the economy is in equilibrium, net output, u, equals the given net demand, $\bar{u}$, and gross output likewise is equal to the amounts demanded. Let all their initial equilibrium values be zero. The change in stocks during any period is $\Delta s_t = \bar{u}_t - \bar{u}$, where s_t is the level of stocks at the beginning and $\bar{u}_t$ is demand, constant throughout the period. Producers set output in period $t+1$ at the level of production last period plus or minus some fraction of their excess or deficiency of stocks at the end of the period compared with their desired level $\bar{s}$, here taken as zero. Therefore

$$q_t + 1 = q_t - \beta s_{t+1} \quad \text{or} \quad \Delta q_t = -\beta s_{t+1}.$$

How and why such a system is bound to overshoot its equilibrium and thus generate a cycle is shown in fig. 6.6. Given demand rises initially from zero to a new, constant level of $\bar{u}$. In some ideal, totally planned economy, gross output could be raised to $\bar{q}$, with inputs at $\bar{a}$, yielding in the same initial period a net output u exactly equal to $\bar{u}$. By contrast in an atomistic, market economy such a change is not foressen and results in a drop in stocks from zero to s_1, equal and opposite to the rise in net demand. β measures the strength of producers' reactions to this unexpected change in stocks; if $\beta = 1$, they produce so as to try to eliminate the deficiency or excess in one step. In reality they appear to react with more caution, making a partial response each time, which may be because of uncertainty about the future course of the demand. Suppose β to be $\frac{1}{2}$, then q_1 will increase to $\frac{1}{2}\bar{u}$. To find the resulting u_1 the scale of output is reduced along the dotted line with the proportion given by q_1. The rise in gross and net output will have reduced the scale and altered the proportions of the discrepancy between given net demand and resulting net output.

Therefore, in period 1, stocks continue to fall, though by less and with some alteration in proportion, to s_2. Though output has narrowed the gap with demand, stocks of both goods have become very low, so output is increased sharply to q_2. This brings net output, u_2, close to net demand, $\bar{u}$ and substantially ends the drain on stocks, only good 2 falling a bit to s_3. Though stocks deficiency is no longer increasing, it remains large, so output is again sharply increased to q_3, lifting net output above net demand and finally bringing about some reduction in the stocks deficiencies to s_4. Here is the crux of the analysis: once stocks are deficient, and they are bound to be whenever change occurs, they can only be rebuilt by raising net output above net demand. But by this very fact gross output has overshot the new equilibrium $\bar{q}'$, as net output has its new equilibrium $\bar{u}$. Though stocks have increased they are still deficient, output is further increased and stocks progress to s_5 and s_6 where only good 2 is deficient. This

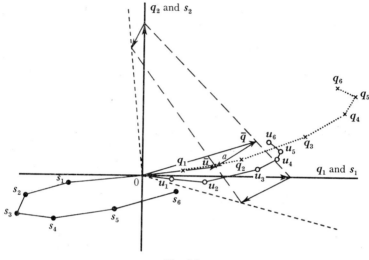

Fig. 6.6

means that the paths of q and u now turn back reducing q_1 whilst q_2 is still increasing, until s arrives in the north-east quadrant with excess of both stocks. Then begins a weak decrease in the output of both goods, which allows both stocks to get still more excessive. In order to eliminate the deficiency in good 2, its output had got very high and so now q and u pass north of their equilibrium points, leading eventually to the right stocks of 1 but excessive for 2. Outputs both fall until both stocks in succession cease rising and then fall. But in order to reduce these, both outputs must now overshoot in the downward direction. Thus a cycle is bound to arise, an inventory, or stocks, cycle. Whether it is stable, with output and stocks each wrapping inwardly onto their equilibrium points, or unstable with each one unwinding in ever greater swings, depends on the whole productive structure and on the sensitivity to stocks imbalance as represented by β. More realistic and more complex assumption about behaviour can be made, but these simple basic relations seem bound to dominate such more complicated models.

6.6. Durable equipment in the short run; 'fixed' costs

In the long run all costs are variable, as they have thus far been treated. But in the short run the fact of the durability of equipment means that some inputs are variable and others, e.g. equipment, are not. In expansion, especially steady expansion, the distinction is not important, though in case of rapid acceleration there may be some delay in expanding equipment. Complications arise in the case of unexpected decelerations or actual contractions. By its very nature durable equipment cannot be reduced rapidly and hence is not freely variable in the downward direction. Up to this point we have been considering steady expansion correctly foreseen. Unfortunately for theory and for reality, expansion is highly unsteady and is commonly not correctly foreseen. Unlike labour and materials durable equipment once installed, has a cost that does not vary in the downward direction when production changes scale, and hence it is a 'fixed' or 'sunk' cost.

The capitalist producer is therefore in a highly vulnerable position: he cannot reduce all his costs with a reduction in output in the face of a reduced demand. This has led to a special sort of behaviour designed to maintain prices in times of low demand. Although price policy varies widely according to market types, the closest approach to a common description of price behaviour goes in terms of a mark-up on variable cost only, such as will lead to covering all costs, including fixed ones, in the long run. The producer aims to install no more equipment than will match demand over the life time of the equipment. He must form an estimate of expected normal demand and will usually have spare capacity to satisfy occasional periods of exceptionally high demand. It is convenient to define the equipment required by a particular process for a given output as an amount which will in fact produce 10 % to 20 % more than the given output. The producer then sets a price as a mark-up $(1+\lambda)$ on variable cost only, high enough to cover all cost, including interest, at the expected normal rate of output. If the output demanded is greater than this, there arises a pure profit, and if lower, a pure loss. For this purpose the common market rate of return on all capital, whether arising out of external debt or from internal funds, must be considered as a cost. It is then a 'full cost' policy which sets a fixed price, regardless of output, but one which will at 'normal' output yield 'normal' profit rate on all invested capital.

A producer has on hand each year a given quantity of equipment, a fraction of which, will cease to function by the end of the period. This fraction, valued at current market price, is the fixed cost of being in existence as a producer, without any output whatsoever. Since a known quantity of equipment will be needed for replacement during the year, it is assumed, not very realistically, that this quantity is purchased at the beginning of the period (as with labour and materials). Then, quite independently of equipment, subject only to feasibility with the given stock of equipment, the producer decides his scale of output for the period, hires the necessary labour and purchases the required raw materials.

The accounting conventions and financial arrangements vary markedly from industry to industry and even firm to firm. Unfortunately these are often arbitrary from an economic point of view. Here it is desirable to adopt one consistent set of conventions, one which is as close as possible to economic logic. Suppose a money market with a single rate of interest, from which the firm can borrow or to which it can lend. There is, of course, the vital difference between short-term borrowing, for one period only, and long-term (debentures or bonds), which is not variable in the downward direction. The amount of this 'fixed' borrowing is not tied to 'fixed' equipment though it tends to be a rather constant portion of it. The remainder of the money capital investment has been supplied by the owners, either in subscribed cash or in retained earnings, in return for an equal shares in the profits. This equity capital can, if desired, be considered as a cost, like debentures, since the owners could have lent it to the market, thus determining its opportunity cost.

Consider the perishable goods industry as a firm, in per capita form as in fig. 6.7. Nominal capacity (80 %, say, of true capacity) may be defined as unit employment (X millions) and the wage rate, w, is the wage bill of X millions for one period. Scale is set by employment, l_h, which may by anything from 0 to $1 \cdot 2$, wage bill being $w l_h$.

The money for this carries an interest cost whether it comes from the market or from internal funds. So that wage cost, for any feasible scale is $l_h(1+r)w$. Similarly for materials, the requirement is $l_h(1+r)\alpha_{hh}$, variable between 1 and 1·2 $(1+r)\alpha_{hh}$ as output varies from 0 to 1·2$\overline{Q}$. The manager is faced with a given technique specified by $\overline{Q}$, α_{hh}, α_{eh}, and θ with given r, w and P_e and has to set a price which will earn a profit of r on all invested capital if output and demand are $\overline{Q}$. The total equipment is $(1+\theta)\alpha_{eh}$ and profit on it is to be $r(1+\theta)\alpha_{eh}$ and its value is its projection on the

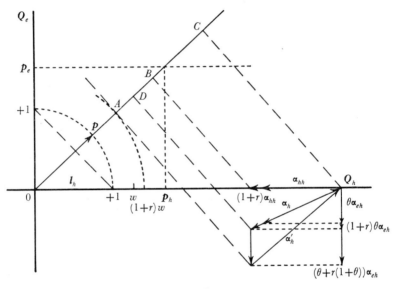

Fig. 6.7

resulting P. Likewise the value of materials must be $(1+r)\alpha_{hh} \cdot P$. The sum of these two values will be the value of their sum or $\alpha_h' \cdot P$. The aim is to set a price such that wage cost, $(1+r)w$, plus all other costs, $\alpha_h' \cdot P$. add to the value of product, $\overline{Q} \cdot P$. From the diagram it is evident that this will be so if P lies on the ray normal to a line drawn from the tip of α_h' and tangent to a circle about the origin of radius $(1+r)w$. Given P_e, its intersection with this P ray determines uniquely P_h. For convenience it is necessary to shrink the price level to P on the unit circle. Then for unit employment and 'normal' output $\overline{Q}$, the value of output is oC, labour cost oA, equipment cost AB, and material cost BC, each inclusive of 'normal' profit. Total revenue equals total cost. Since oA and BC and oC all vary proportionately with output, the same ratios hold for all outputs including unit. For unit output oC is price, oA unit labour cost and BC unit material cost, so that mark-up is given by $\lambda = oc/(oA + BC) - 1$. It is immediately evident that such a mark-up will be different in every industry depending on the widely differing importance of equipment in the cost structure.

Operating profit, $(AB)l_h$, is the extra revenue obtained by operating at any scale, l_h, rather than not operating at all. AB itself is the cost of the fixed capital equipment and the proportion of fixed cost covered by operating profit is given by l_h for any feasible scale of operation. It is a question of convenience and practice as to whether 'normal' profits are to to be considered a cost or not. Replacement cost, BD, is properly a cost, so that only when l_h is greater than BD/AB, does the industry earn any return on fixed capital investment. From the point of view of the owners, any contractual fixed interest (e.g. bonds) is a cost so that some portion of AD may be added to BD to define the scale at which profit appears. Or AB itself may be considered as the most logical measure of the total capital cost, though this is not common practice. However defined the scale at which operating profit equals fixed cost is called the 'break-even point' and is of considerable practical significance in decisions about price and about provision for added capacity and equipment.

In the long run normal equilibrium, if such a state is ever achieved, the two methods of mark-up achieve the same result—a common rate of profit in all industries. In the short run they differ considerably. Full cost mark-up is a defence against price competition in time of low demand. It is, however, an ambiguous name, since it is only full cost at one level of output, a level rarely if ever achieved. At lower output pure losses appear and at higher outputs pure profits, pure in the sense of being higher or lower than the generality of profit rates. If it were truly a full cost principle, prices would have to be raised in times of low demand and lowered in times of high demand—neither of which appeals to producers. The fixed mark-up is no doubt a rule-of-thumb way of allowing for the uncertainty of demand in laying down and pricing the products of durable equipment. It avoids the complexities of more sophisticated probabilistic calculations, and, if managers follow the simpler path, we may gratefully follow their example.

This analysis shows why company profits are so very sensitive to fluctuations in demand. Replacement plus contractual debt may make up a large proportion of operating profit. Output only needs to fall to this proportion of normal for net profits to be reduced to zero. If replacement plus contractual debt were to make up 90 % of 'normal' operating profit, then a rise of output by only 10 % above normal would raise net profits by 100 %.

6.7. Income generation in a growing economy

The essential logic of the Kahn–Keynes Multipliers may be expressed as follows: for a stationary equilibrium effective demand must be neither rising nor falling; receipts in one period lead to a somewhat smaller outlay the next; on the other hand these are outlays that do not arise from previous receipts; the gap between receipts and outlays must be made up by the outlays that do not arise from receipts, if outlay is not to rise or fall from period to period; if we call the gap saving and the autonomous outlays investment, we get the proposition that savings must equal investment.

To see the application of this to the situation of section 6 above, it is helpful to make some rather exteme simplifications. Households spend all they receive on consumption, so that all saving is done by companies. Of the receipts of a company, some is spent for wage cost, some for material, replacement of equipment (on the assumption that allowance for depreciation and actual disappearance of equipment are the same). The remainder of receipts is operating profit, which, less fixed interest payments, is net profit, less dividends paid out, is company saving. All these items except company saving, are purchases of goods and services (and hence receipts by others) or are payments to households, where they are totally spent as purchases. Thus receipts = $receipts_{t+1}$ – company saving. If autonomous expenditure, e.g. investments outlay, equals company saving, the $receipts_t$ = $receipts_{t+1}$ and stationary equilibrium holds.

Suppose in fig. 6.7 that industry h is the whole economy. The amount of equipment in existence is $(1+\theta)a_{eh}$, some part, say half of which has been purchased by fixed interest loans. The firms then have two fixed charges against operating profits, $l_h(AB)$, $\frac{1}{2}AD+DB$. The net profits available for dividends or for ploughing back are, then, $l_h(AB)-(\frac{1}{2}AD+DB)$. These net profits are either retained or paid out as dividends, the criterion for doing which is very important but does not seem to carry much economic logic with it. The criteria for determining dividends are many and various but the underlying aim seems to be to smooth out the rather wide fluctuations in net profits. Thus if profits are low in one year, dividends will be little reduced but if they continue to be low, dividends are gradually reduced correspondingly. To simplify, however, assume that dividends are simply half net profits. In terms of fig. 6.7 retained earnings or company saving becomes $\frac{1}{2}[l_hAB-\frac{1}{2}AD-DB]$. If producers are spending an amount of value AG on expansion, for equilibrium, the scale of output, l_h, must be such the the expression in brackets is twice the outlay on expansion. If there is no expansion, $l_h = \frac{1}{2}(AD+DB)/AB$ about 75 % in the example. The maximum outlay on expansion would be about $\frac{1}{5}$ if l_h can be no larger than $1\cdot2$. Thus investment determines net profits which are simply a multiple of them; it also determines company saving which is equal in amount and supplies the finance for the investment. But this is not because profits or finance control or limit investment; the causation runs the other way and it does so through income generation. So long as investment is greater than company saving, receipts will be rising, or so long as it is lower, receipts will be falling. Investment controls the level of gross receipts and hence of output, and hence of employment and of net output as well. The existence of saving out of wages, dividends and interest complicates and softens the argument but does not alter its general tenor.

The crisp outline of the Keynesian analysis conceals beneath the surface some large and awkward questions. Equilibrium means stationary conditions with constant aggregate monetary demand both gross and net. But if capacity and output are continually being expanded, the resulting output can only be sold at a falling price level. However, we have just seen that the operation of a capitalist mark-up price policy is precisely designed to maintain prices constant in such a case and allow output to fall instead.

This is the Marxian realization problem: can capitalists with their desire to save and accumulate, dispose of the increasing quantities of goods they produce? The problem once clearly formulated suggests its own answer: yes, they can if they accumulate on precisely the right, ever-increasing, scale. But it has only to be stated to make it plain how unlikely it is to happen in a free capitalist market system, especially when properly formulated in a disaggregated structure. If they accumulate too rapidly, demand will exceed output available and stocks decline. This would predictably lead them to a further expansion of accumulation and only make matters worse. If on the other hand they are expanding too slowly, output exceeds demand and stocks accumulate, so they would further restrict expansion to reduce stocks, the result of which instead is to accelerate the growth of unwanted stocks. The persistent instability of capitalist expansion is surely related to this uncomfortable situation.

It will be noted that a subtle change of emphasis has occurred here. This is a system whose only equilibrium is not stationary but only semi-stationary, i.e. output and employment are increasing, output per head and prices are constant. Total outlay and demand must be increasing for equilibrium, so that the equilibrium requires autonomous outlay (investment) to be greater than saving (whether company or personal). Apparently contradictory, this can be reconciled with the foregoing analysis by recalling it is investment outlay that is being equated with saving out of this year's output but it is being spent on the goods not consumed out of last year's (smaller) output. There are also important implications for stability. If investment had to equal saving, it is conceivable that an efficient and properly organized money market could channel the flow of savings to investors and thus limit investment outlay to available funds, which could guarantee equilibrium even in an atomistic economy. But with an equilibrium condition that investment be larger by a precise amount than saving, it is quite inconceivable that any kind of atomistic system would ever arrive at the creation of just the right amount of new money and new money capital.

Once the two sectors have accumulated a particular pair of stocks of durables, they will each have both fixed and variable capital charges. The fixed charge consists of interest payments to households, which is in turn fully spent on goods, represented by *GH* in fig. 6.8. Then total demand consists of demand equal in value to the wage bill plus interest payments plus dividends, along with producer demands for inputs.

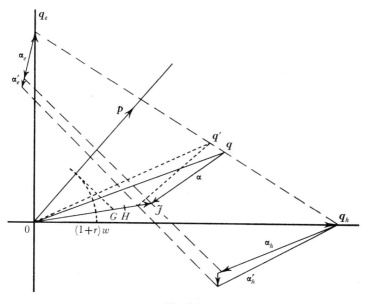

Fig. 6.8

First, consider the case of zero expansion: what will be the equilibrium level of output? Let unit sum of employment correspond to nominal capacity. An excess of net output over wage bill must be produced large enough to cover the fixed interest demand *GH*. There will be no net profit, hence no dividends and no consumption arising. The scale of employment, measured by the length of l, must be such as to reduce net profits *GJ*, to fixed interest outlay, *GH*. o*G* and α both contract with scale, only *GH* remains constant and determines the scale of output.

Any positive rate of expansion will increase demand and bring a higher level of employment. The demand for inputs is increased by the expanded scale of production. In addition profits result in dividends payments which in turn result in consumption. The locus of u' must run through the middle of the stretch *HJ* if one half of profits lead to consumption. Not only is the scale of output greater but its composition is altered from q to q' in favour of e since the added demands are mostly for e. Evidently each growth rate will be associated with a level of output and employment. The two growth rates need not be equal; all that is required is that, for equilibrium, the output must generate a level of demand equal to itself. Section 6.8 is devoted to a fuller account of this relation.

6.8. Income generation with both fixed and variable consumption feed-back

The argument of section 6.2 is correct but incomplete in that it ignores the fact that variations in output give rise to variations in income which in turn change consumption demand and hence output. This is the specifically Keynesian factor in output determination. In order not to get lost in the intricacies of disaggregated national accounting, it is desirable to make a few simplifications, simplifications which do not seriously distort the central features of the analysis. Assume prices are determined by mark-up so that at nominal full capacity operation full cost is covered. This nominal capacity, with given techniques, gives rise to unit employment, i.e. $l_e + l_h = 1$. Firms always replace equipment, which being given in amount represents a fixed cost and a fixed subtraction from gross output. Gross outputs and inputs of goods are variable with the level of employment. The value of net output less wages paid out less fixed interest at the market rate on the stocks of equipment, constitutes profits. Dividends are some constant fraction, say two-thirds of profits. All income paid out, as distinct from earned, is spent in a common fixed set of proportions on consumer goods. Disposable income consists of wages, plus interest on equipment, plus dividends. Interest on working capital is ignored. The stock of consumer durables, like that of producers, is given independently of demand. Interest payments on it are ignored. These conditions suffice to determine, for income and employment, an equilibrium point which equates supply and demand for goods.

Call unit sum employment, $L = 1$, that amount which results from nominal capacity output, Q. Fixed replacement outlay, $\alpha_e \cdot p = F_R$, may be added to fixed interest payments to give total fixed outlay, F. Wages cost at $L = 1$, is $W = w$, the wage rate for employing that number of workers. Let $U'' = Q - \alpha_h$; then $U'' \cdot p$ in fig. 6.9 gives the operating revenue available for fixed outlays plus wages cost. Nominal capacity operation then produces a total profit of $\Pi = U'' \cdot p - W - F$.

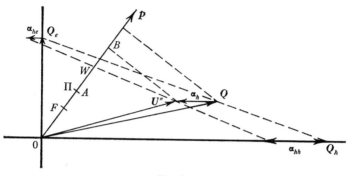

Fig. 6.9

Operating revenue $U'' \cdot p$ will vary with the composition of output but once proportions are determined, variations in scale, $l/L = l$, in equal proportion will affect the variable quantities, Q, U'', W, as well as $Q.P$ and $U'' \cdot P$. For any scale of operation, l, the wage bill will be lW and operating revenue will be $l(U'' \cdot P)$, so that value of product less wage and materials cost for any scale of output will be $l(U'' \cdot P - W) = l(0A)$. Against this must be set fixed outlays, F, leaving profits as the difference. The sensitivity of profits to variations in scale is evident. For operation under capacity, $l < 1$; $l(0A)$ shrinks on to F and profits disappear and for $l > 1$, profits soar into the super normal. Thus if $\Pi = 10$ and $F = 30$, profit becomes zero at 83% of capacity and becomes 160% of full cost, or normal, profit at only 110% of capacity.

Equilibrium conditions for scale and proportions may be separated. Take first the case of no net investment. For unit scale the value of aggregate output is $Q \cdot p$; this entails a demand of $\alpha_h \cdot P$ for inputs, of W from the wages bill, of F from fixed outlays and of two-thirds of profits from dividends, but there is no demand corresponding to the remaining one-third of profits, which corresponds to a similar value of output. Therefore for aggregate demand to equal aggregate supply, the scale of output must be reduced until profits are zero, i.e. l must fall until $l(Q \cdot p - \alpha_h \cdot p - W) = F$, regardless of what share of profits are disbursed as dividends. Net investment being zero, net saving, and hence profits also, must be zero. With given technique and a given Q, outlay on wages and materials constitute a fixed proportion of the value of gross product and hence

$$l(Q \cdot p) = \frac{1}{1 - \dfrac{\alpha_h \cdot p}{Q \cdot p} - w/Q \cdot p} F$$

giving an aggregate multiplier which is constant. The scale of output, l, is proportional to the level of given outlays, F. Thus short-run rigidities prop up the economy, rigidities which would disappear in the long run, the replacements not effected, the fixed interest dissolved by repayment or bankruptcy. The only long-run equilibrium with zero investment is zero output and income. In this short-run model, the profits share in output, being only spent for goods in a fixed proportion, has to be reduced to zero. In fact most companies tend to smooth profit fluctuations by disbursing dividends partly in fixed quantity and partly variable. Similarly, householders have fixed commitments so that they do not reduce expenditure as much as disposable income falls. Adding these assumptions complicates the analysis but does not basically alter it. Likewise rigidities inhibit expansion—capacity limits, fixed costs leading to supernormal profits, and saving. Saving limits the demand unless balanced by net investment but super-normal investment leads to the dissolution of the rigidities in the form of higher capacity, greater fixed interest and the like.

Assuming that there is a clear distinction between net and replacement investment, a distinction far from clear in reality, there exists a given net demand for new equipment, regardless of which sector originates the demand, which, valued at P_e means a third type of given outlay, i.e. $F = F_r + F_R + F_{N'}$, fixed interest, fixed replacement and fixed net accumulation. Although F_N is a given outlay independent of scale, it functions differently because it does not enter into calculation of profits. The total value of output is $\alpha_h \cdot P + F_r + F_N + W + \Pi$; the first four of these items represent at the same time shares in value of product and the same shares in the demand for product. This leaves only Π as a share of product to be accounted for, but Π only gives rise to demand for product of $\frac{2}{3}\Pi$, so that, if all the product is to be demanded, F_N must constitute the remaining share of demand, thus

$$\tfrac{2}{3}\Pi + F_N = \Pi,$$

or

$$\Pi = 3F_N.$$

Therefore aggregative equilibrium exists when l is such that $l(U'' \cdot P - W)$ reduces or expands to $3F_N$. In fig. 6.9 this requires that $l(oA) = F + 3F_N$.

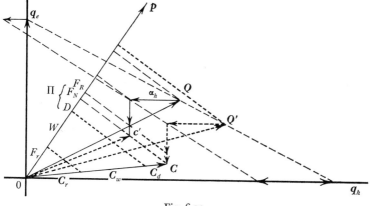

Fig. 6.10

In aggregative equilibrium, Say's Law is satisfied; total demand equals total supply but individual sectors may or may not be in a similar equilibrium. It is of great importance that demand for consumption comes from disposable income and it does not matter in which sector the income originates. This large segment of demand being common to all sectors undoubtedly explains why all sectors, in the short run, tend to move up and down roughly in step. But there are exceptions and vagaries of individual sectors and it is to this problem that we now come—the determination of proportions, given scale.

With scale determined by aggregate effective demand, employment, output, input of materials and wages can be proportionally scaled up or down as in fig. 6.10. All consumption is in a common proportion and is divided into three parts

$$C_r, \ C_w, \ C_D; \ C_r \cdot P = F_r; \ C_w \cdot P = W;$$
$$C_D \cdot P = D; \ D + F_N = \Pi; \ F_N + F_R$$

are the values of given gross investment; all these plus $\alpha_h \cdot P$ add to the value of output $Q \cdot P$ and Say is satisfied.

The scale of Q has been determined but not its proportions. Thus in fig. 6.10 the goods available for consumption are C' and the goods demanded are C; aggregate demand for consumption equals aggregate supply, but more h is demanded than supplied and less e. Alteration of the composition, but not of the scale, of output is required to bring C' into approximate equality with C in detail as well as in aggregate. A secondary re-calculation becomes necessary since the value of output and of variable inputs alter with changes in composition. This in turn leads to a further small change in consumption which then requires a further recalculation and so on until substantial equality of supply and demand in detail is found.

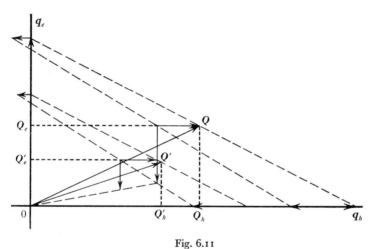

Fig. 6.11

A variation in F_r and hence C_r will lead mainly to a change of scale, but a change in net investment outlay, F_N, has dramatic effect not only on scale but on proportions, and it is principally F_N that changes in the short run. Fig. 6.11 suggests roughly the nature of the effect of a decline by 50 % in gross investment. The primary impact is solely on the equipment sector, but this has a secondary impact on aggregate demand, especially through consumption. First, the workers are laid off in e leading to a fall in demand for both goods, which leads to a tertiary decline in employment and consumption of both goods and so on until the given demands, which do not fall, bring a ceasation of the decline in scale. But an important shift in proportion has occurred; the output of e has fallen to about 50 % of capacity whereas that of h to about 80 %. This dissimilar behaviour of the two types of industry characterizes most slumps.

With this type of model it is evident that we can proceed to introduce fiscal behaviour and policy. Taxes on personal income, profits or turnover can be introduced; transfer payments to house-holders, government current expenditure and investment can be added as well as interest payments on government securities. These can be manipulated to construe the effects of a given policy or to formulate a policy with a given desired result.

6.9. The vagaries of capitalist growth

With the various elements added the model has become quite complicated in its behaviour. Even so it cannot be expected to get very close to actual economic behaviour, but it is important to investigate how completely it can offer explanations for a number of central features of reality. The most important elements in the action of the economy (and it is only by observing change that the interconnections of a system can be found) seem to be that there is a roughly constant, given growth in labour force, that plant and equipment are producible on any scale, that the output is determined by these plus a slow change in the known technology. These things are the aggregate product of vast numbers of small independent events and as such tend to be smooth, even development, but what has never been steady, in capitalist evolution, is the actual output, employment and rate of growth of durable equipment.

It is more or less unavoidable that, somehow or other, equipment must adapt to labour force, subject to the best methods according to the current technology. The aim is to see how satisfactorily such a model can explain the character and irregularity of this adaption process.

At any given time, with the real wage rate then ruling, there will be for each sector a best technique which it will be operating, or at least be in the process of converting to. This determines a ratio between employment of equipment and of labour whatever the level of output.

If, as is bound to happen from time to time, equipment fails to grow with labour force, so that there are unemployed workers not matched by unemployed equipment, then, if, as also happens, the economy regains approximate full employment of labour, the accumulation of e must proceed at a greater rate than that of labour. Consequently, in the neighbourhood of full employment, rupture of this growth path is bound to occur. Accumulation must be decelerated to the range of labour force plus productivity growth. But if the rate of accumulation is cut, the level of output must fall and there is no reason to accumulate at all, so that a dramatic crisis of greater or less severity is bound to ensue. The difficulty is signalled by rising money wages; real wages may or may not rise, with a resulting fall in profit rates, but whether they do or not, the real problem remains. The evasion or softening of the problem explains the great importance of supplementary sources of cheap labour to capitalism, e.g. immigration from low wage countries or low wage industries like agriculture. Ultimately, however, it is impossible to continue staffing facilities expanding at the previous high rate. As is abundantly evident from section 6.8, the rate of accumulation is the prime determinant of the level of output. Therefore a slackening of the rate of accumulation, means an actual fall in the scale of output.

This awkward relation means in the simplest sense that all net accumulation should cease and some or all replacement also. In the absence of fixed outlays, everything would go to zero, which certainly does not happen. In fact rarely if ever does even net accumulation go to zero. The reasons are not too clear but disaggregation helps. A fall in investment alters the composition of output as much as its scale since the main blow falls on the durable goods, but they only make up, say, 15 to 20 % of output, so that even if its output falls to 50 %, there will only be an over-all fall of 5 to 10 %. The e sector will certainly stop expanding but it may not allow a run-down of its capacity since, from past experience, it is known that a subsequent recovery will induce an equally violent expansion of demand. In any case e's purchases of its own product are rather small, so that it comes down to the behaviour of h sector. Its sales have only declined a very modest amount and this only from the level it would have reached had the expansion been able to continue, so that it may only suffer a lower growth rate rather than actual decline. Or sales may decline and there may be some, but not much failure to replace equipment. There is a great variety of possibilities and all such events vary. Purely for simplicity assume that in the aggregate net accumulation ceases but that replacement continues. This means that net saving must go to zero, and that profits must also, if savings are some fixed proportion of profits. In section 6.8 it has been shown that due to the heavy fixed charges, profits are extremely vulnerable to small variations in sales. Therefore to reduce profits to zero does not require a very heavy fall in output. Also very important is the asymmetry in wage behaviour; wages rise with low unemployment but do not fall, or fall very little, with higher unemployment. If wages fell, this would hold up profits and force a still greater fall in output and employment to reduce savings from profits to the level of accumulation.

The modest fall in aggregate output conceals a large shift in its composition; there is a drastic fall in a small sector, e, and a mild fall in the large sector, h, along with heavy losses in e and modest profits in h. Thus suddenly the economy grinds to a halt in its growth. The suddenness, many times observed, seems inherent in the nature of growth in an atomistic, market-controlled economy. Though the onset is dramatic the effects take some time to work out since they proceed in successively smaller downward lurches as each sector's reaction affects the others and so on. Stocks behaviour also at first softens the blow and then magnifies it; to begin with, output (and demand) remain higher than sales so that stocks build up; but then to unload the stocks, output (and demand) are pushed below sales, thus carrying the economy even lower than need be.

Output and employment are constant, profits are zero and unemployment grows. It is important to realize that though profits have disappeared, there is nothing essentially unprofitable about production; it is merely that the operating profits are absorbed by the costs of an over-built capacity that is unusable at the time. Profits are zero because accumulation is. The profit rate has not altered since real wages have not. Profit is not zero because wages are absorbing the whole product; the reduced product is being shared between wages and fixed, contractual profit (interest). The mark-up has presumably not altered; the scale of output has simply gone below 'normal', the break-even point. Thus a new enterprize would, operating at nominal capacity, earn normal profits. The question arises whether or not companies could settle down comfortably at this low level of operation. The answer is no. They would gradually reduce capacity, contractual debt and any dividends not covered by profits, but then output and demand would proceed to a still lower level and the process would begin all over again.

Therefore, though exceptionally difficult, it is not as unlikely as at first it seems, that new enterprizes may be started. Thus a shift from coal to electricity would lead to large outlays for new generating plant, which would be normally profitable. This would not lead to a reduction in contractual interest in coal though it almost certainly would lead to a reduction in outlays for the replacement equipment. More important is the development of commercially feasible production of a new product which succeeds in diverting demand from established products. Equally it could be a new process for producing an old product though here the test is more severe: it must be productive enough to make its current plus capital costs less than the current costs alone in the existing process.

In any case the net investment does arise; it always has. Capitalism has been characterized by a restless search for new and profitable activities to exploit. Only in the 1870's and in the 1930's did it seem to have lost this quality. The resulting outlays for e will have its various mutliple effects as determined by the productive structure (section 6.2). As these various sectors increase their outputs, two further things happen: wages payments rise leading to a further pattern of increased demand, providing a common ground-swell regardless of the origin of the wages. Secondly, there is a stocks effect which will raise output, after a lag, by more than the rise in demand, so that there is a further upward leverage. The critical question is whether or not the combined effect is sufficient to raise output to nominal capacity in the bulk of sectors. If not the upsurge will be abortive, but if so then the producers will undertake some net expansion of capacity, which again, but more massively because more general, will have multiple effects on demand, output and employment. Proceeding thus the economy will regain the previous high levels of accumulation, super-normal levels of output and profits. These new installations will incorporate the technical progress which has accrued but not been utilized. Therefore, at this point, no problems of labour supply arises because of lower labour requirements and because of the growth in the labour force.

There is no reason to expect the growth rates in the various sectors to be the same, though they will mostly be under the common influence of consumer demand. The growth rate of capacity in e might be expected to be higher since its demand rises fastest. However, its vulnerability to slight shifts in growth rate means that it tends to expand only cautiously and not in step with demand, allowing, rather, a back-log of orders to develop. The situation is soon reached in which there is general full employment of equipment whilst labour remains in excess supply. Then output growth is limited not by demand, but by the rate of growth of equipment as determined by capacity output in e. In this state the economy is rather invulnerable to moderate disturbances. Perishable goods are being produced at peak-load and want more capacity than they possess, so that if there are temporary lapses in growth of demand, they will not react by cutting their expansion programmes. And even if some companies do reduce expansion, this only shortens the queue for equipment. The output of e founded on their back-log, remains constant or slowly rises and hence aggregate output (and employment) rises at a constant rate or slowly accelerates.

Proceeding thus, the economy arrives eventually at simultaneous full employment of equipment and of labour; the smooth progress is broken and the transient breakdown recurs. At the full employment points the economy is in the same condition it would be in were it to be experiencing golden age, steady growth. It will take longer to reach these points but it does get there and it does so by alternating, first a growth rate above the steady rate, and then a growth rate below it.

This analysis gives the clue to the answer to the question of why, in the long run, there tends to be (a) constant shares, (b) rising wage rates and constant profit rates. This result is by no means obviously necessary, particularly since, in a capitalist system, the fruits of technical progress accrue to the capitalists in the form of lower costs and higher profits. A simple answer would be that by keeping a constant mark-up, the gain is passed on to labour in the form of lower prices. In fact this does not happen and would be irrational behaviour in a capitalist mark-up which is primarily designed to hold up prices when demand falls and to put up prices when costs rise. When a new labour-saving process is gradually introduced in an industry it leads to a higher profit rate. This allows that industry to grow faster than others and/or to pay higher wages, and thus bidding away labour in a tightening labour market. Given time the other industries will tend to alter either prices or techniques so that they can pay these same wages and earn the same profit rate. The new common profit rate may be either at the old or the new rate or anywhere in between.

If the common profit rate is raised by the succession of improvements with technology, then during the boom phase, profits will be higher, savings higher with a greater rate of accumulation and of growth in output and employment. Consequently the full employment peak will be attained sooner, with the boom phase shorter relative to the depressed phase. The important point is that once there it has regained the steady growth path and, apart from time, is superficially indistinguishable from an economy that has followed the steady path. If we call the previous peak output a and the current one b, then to get from q_a to q_b has meant the same accumulation of e, the same savings, the same profit rate, and the same increase in employment in the two cases. The rate of profit and of accumulation and of growth, taken as the percentage increase in b over a, will be the same. Thus the aggregate and average annual behaviours of the profit rate will be independent of the current profit rate, by means of altering the proportion of time spent at high and at low profits. What is affected is wages, for the fact that output has been below full employment, that the labour output capacity during those years has been forever wasted, must come from somewhere over the period from a to b, the output of equipment is the same but not the output of consumer goods. The wages were not paid; the consumption goods were not produced; the low output was at the expense of the worker.

As the expansion proceeds it becomes increasingly difficult to secure labour and money wages rise. The sectors which have been carrying out technical innovation can pay the higher wages without raising prices whilst the others must partly raise prices and partly alter their technique in favour of the known labour-saving methods. Thus real wages rise since all prices do not rise in proportion to the rise in money wages. Thus it is in consequence of the competition for scarce labour that real wages rise. The rise in real wages can take place without a diminution in the high rate of accumulation because of the rise in labour productivity. The secondary shake-out of labour in unprogressive sectors postpones the tightness of the labour market without removing it eventually. Therefore when the peak is reached real wages will have risen in spite of high prices and high accumulation.

When the relapse occurs, money wages rates fall little if at all (though the wage bill falls heavily) and prices do not go up as would be required by a short-run full cost policy, so that the gain in real wage rates is preserved. The extent of the fall in output and employment is cushioned not only by the high wage rates but by the large fixed interest and dividend payment built up during the period of rapid accumulation. In the ensuing boom, when it comes, profits in some sectors will again be high because of the introduction of the newer more productive techniques. Until labour shortage appears, these high profits may endure but this only leads to a more rapid approach to the tight labour market which will lead to higher real wage rates. By contrast, profit rates, taking good years and bad years together over the whole stretch from peak to peak, will be constant from cycle to cycle. This appears to offer an explanation of the fact that profit rates show no secular tendency to rise whereas wage rates quite clearly do. It also offers an explanation of why, in spite of this basically different behaviour, the share of profits, and hence wages, tends to constancy in the long run.

7

INTRODUCTION TO DYNAMIC PROGRAMMING

It is evident that economic analysis relies heavily on the technique of optimizing, usually in the form of maximizing. This is so for normative economics where a maximum represents the goal and a standard by which performance may be judged. Descriptive or positive economic analysis may also use the methods of optimality in the form of the rational household or firm behaving in such a way as to maximize something. In both cases this is usually considered for a single period of time, but in reality these periods are not isolated since they are interrelated, most obviously where durable goods are involved. Therefore it is necessary to maximize not merely within a single period but over many, even infinitely many, periods. The resulting analytic problem can become extremely complex. All that can be done here is to provide an introduction to the subject which will illustrate the nature of some of the problems and the results. To do this requires severely simplified assumptions which, it is to be hoped, avoid the details without losing the essentials.

In a dynamic system there exist linkages which, given the initial position, determine a unique evolution over time. The system may be disturbed by influences outside the system which, in effect constitute a new initial position at the time of impact, and hence alter the evolution. A system may have, however, one or more variable quantities which are not determined, giving rise to a choice of behaviour. The quantities open to choice are called control variables, and the others, which describe the position of the system, are called state variables. The system, in such a case, can be dynamically programmed, by proper choice of control variables, to perform a prescribed, feasible manoeuvre in time. If the prescription is not specific but rather a requirement that some evaluation of its behaviour be maximized or minimized, then it is a case of optimal dynamic programming.

7.1. Optimal accumulation with unemployment

There are two basic elements in the problem: the given technical possibilities for shifting output from one period to another and the valuation criteria for assessing which of the possible outcomes is best. The main problem is one of determining the scale of output at various points and therefore, in the interest of getting a clear picture of the analysis, it is desirable to consider aggregates, even though there are important implications for the composition of output and some limitations arising therefrom.

Imagine an economy with a constant labour force but some unemployment. It is desired to increase output and employment over a given number of periods by reducing consumption first, and thus accumulating equipment, and, consequently, raising consumption in the later periods. This may be done in a great variety of shapes and degrees. To choose the best there must be a valuation procedure. Suppose it to be the simplest: the sum of consumption over the whole set of periods must be a maximum.

By not consuming, current output may take the form of durable goods which will then be available as capacity to increase output later and this greater output may then be consumed. How much greater naturally depends on the techniques into which the new accumulation is put. Suppose that somehow a best technique has been chosen (*vide* section 5.6) in which 4 units of output accumulated as equipment raise capacity by 1 unit, assuming, for simplicity, that the durable equipment lasts forever. Therefore by consuming one less unit this year, they can consume $1\frac{1}{4}$ units next year, thus raising the sum of consumption for the two years. But such problems can never be solved by isolated pairs of years, for next year the same problem poses itself—shall the $1\frac{1}{4}$ units be consumed? The answer is no, of course, since by not consuming it, 25 % more can be consumed the following year. And so it goes, never jam today, always jam tomorrow because there will be more gain, until the terminal plan year, when all the gain is consumed in one glorious binge. Not only do they put off any single act of consumption from year to year, they put off all consumption altogether, since any consumption can always be increased by postponing it. That this is economic nonsense should not blind us to the fact that it is a valid and correct optimal dynamic programme, of a rather common type, known as bang-bang. Thus in rocketry dynamic programming has revealed that, to lift a given weight to maximum height or a maximum weight to a given height, the motors must operate at full thrust and then cut out; there is no easing in and easing out, etc.

The fault lies not in the analysis but in the formulation, in particular in the valuation: one unit of consumption is not of equal value to another regardless of the amounts consumed with it. A somewhat more sensible result would follow if consumption over and above some minimal standard, is maximized, but this still does not help much; the community would lead a miserable life for some years, and not be recompensed in one final good year. Obviously the transfer of a unit of consumption from the final year to any previous year would be preferable. An optimal programme requires all possible shifts in consumption to be made so long as they are preferred. When no further feasible shift is preferred, the optimal programme has been found. To make this more precise it is convenient to assign numbers to the amount of consumption for each year in such a way that if the sum of the number for one set of consumptions is greater than that for a different set, it is preferred. The problem then becomes one of making the sum of valuations as great as possible. This valuation may be called utility so long as it is remembered that utility is merely a method of discovering preferences and has no substantial existence in its own right. The fundamental quality of utility is that more consumption is preferred to less but that the strength of this preference decreases with increasing consumption, i.e. the marginal utility of consumption is always decreasing with increasing consumption.

Although very difficult to achieve in practice, assume that a utility function of consumption is determined somehow. From this a marginal utility function $\Delta U(C_t)$, is derived, as represented in fig. 7.1. From this it is easy to see the condition that the time series of consumption must fulfil. If a unit of consumption in year t can always be converted to $1\cdot25$ units in year $t+1$, then the marginal utility of consumption in year t must be $1\cdot25$ times as large as that in year $t+1$, which must be just that much larger to make this so, i.e. $[1\cdot25\Delta C]\Delta U(C_{t+1}) = [\Delta C]\Delta U(C_t)$. If there is to be no preference for a further shift in consumption, the areas (valuations) of the two columns must be equal, which requires the height of the first to be as much larger than that of the second as the base of the second is of the first. More generally if the input coefficient for equipment is a_e then $\Delta U(C_t)/\Delta U(C_{t+1}) = 1 + 1/a_e$. Thus successive marginal utilities all bear the same constant ratio to one another, no matter where we start or finish. This implies a constant rate of decrease of marginal utility equal to the output-equipment ratio, i.e.

$$\frac{\Delta U(C_{t+1}) - \Delta U(C_t)}{\Delta U(C_{t+1})} = 1/a_e.$$

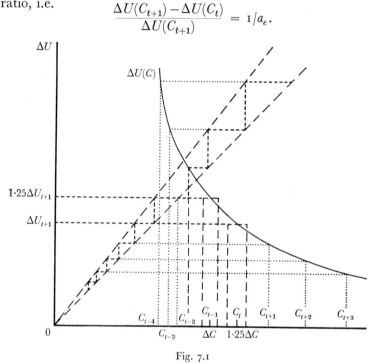

Fig. 7.1

This result may be called Ramsey's Rule after its discoverer. Once any one consumption is chosen, all other consumptions are determined and the optimal time path determined. This can be seen easily from the diagram by placing a 45° line (slope 1) and above it a line with slope $1 + 1/a_e$ (in this case 1·25). Thus for any consumption and its marginal utility, we can find the marginal utility 1·25 as large and from that what the previous year's consumption must be. This relationship is reversible in time; it can go, for example, from C_5 to C_{10} or from C_8 to C_4.

The problem, then, is to find what the consumption must be for any one year. A reduction of consumption in one year results in increased output the next year and hence in no way resolves the problem, since again the same problem arises. Thus we are driven forward, with an unresolved set of choices, to the terminal period where, usually, there is some given condition which must be fulfilled. With this the problem can then be solved in reverse order, from year to year, to the initial situation. Thus the whole programme must be solved simultaneously. The fact that there is no way of isolating and solving by binary pairs of years explains why no market mechanism can ever be expected even to approximate the optimal solution. Markets operate on current and expected prices but these expected prices turn out to be based, necessarily, on past information. What is required for optimal programming is not simply past performance but a complete specification of the behaviour all the way to the end of the plan period.

Therefore the problem is, given initial and terminal conditions, the dynamic optimality conditions must bridge the gap between each stage, so that when each step changes in such a way that both sets of conditions are fulfilled, the problem is solved. The set of quantities which describe the situation at any point of time are the state variables; the control variables must determine the evolution of the state of the system to achieve optimality.

Almost all economic variables must be positive or zero and, in this particular example with permanent durables, consumption, the control variable can never be greater than output. It is usual to assume that there is an absolute minimum to consumption, either subsistence or conventional, at the approach to which marginal utility grows without limit. Initial output is limited by, and must surely be at, its upper limit, as determined by the existing stock of durable equipment. Therefore initial consumption must lie between its minimum, giving maximal accumulation, and output, with no growth at all. Each initial consumption once chosen, will determine a growth curve of consumption over the whole period. The lower we place consumption originally the faster it will grow, making for a preferable situation later. On the other hand by having a higher, and preferable, consumption earlier, we have a less attractive future.

Since equipment is the only scarce input, it will always be fully utilized, so that e_t always will equal $a_e q_t$ and hence q_t is the only state variable needed. The population being constant, it does not matter whether output is per capita or not. Over a given number of years, T, the sum of valuations of consumption is to be maximized. It will be obvious, given this objective, that consumption in the terminal year must equal output, else we could increase $U(C_T)$ without reducing any other year's valuation. Hence $C_T = q_T$ but neither is given, so it may appear that there is no terminal condition. In fact it is impicit in our objective, since if $C_T = q_T$, $\Delta q_T = 0$, so a terminal zero rate of growth has been specified. Because the same productive relationship governs output and marginal utility optimality, the same diagram as before may be used with a line of slope 1 and above it a line of slope $1 + 1/a_e$. The economy is completely specified by

$$q_t = C_t + \triangle e$$
$$= C_t + a_e q_{t+1} - a_e q_t,$$
or
$$q_{t+1} = (1 + 1/a_e) q_t - 1/a_e C_t.$$

If q_T is known, C_T is, but having C_T, C_{T-1} can be found, and having that, with q_T, q_{T-1} is determined. Then to C_{T-2}, and so on regressing in time until $q_{T-T} = q_0$ is reached, which is given. Therefore $q_T = C_T$ is determined by dynamical optimality plus q_0. If there is an explicit function $\Delta U(C)$, the problem can be solved by writing out q_T as a function of q_0, or if it is given only graphically as in fig. 7.2 it can be solved by trial and error.

Once q_T is found, the optimal path from q_0, C_0 to q_T, C_T can be traced. From C_T follows C_{T-1}, and $1/a_e C_{T-1} = (1 + 1/a_e) C_T - C_T$. q_T must be such that $(1 + 1/a_e) q_{T-1}$ less $1/a_e C_{T-1}$ is equal to q_T. This is found by extending a line parallel to the upper line from the point $C_{T-1} = C_{T-1}$ until it reaches the height of q_T; q_{T-1} lies then directly below it. Thus from C_{T-1}, C_{T-2} is found and with q_{T-1}; q_{T-2} is located in the same way. Regressing thus in T steps, q_0 and C_0 are determined along with all the intermediate values. If it is found that q_{T-T} is greater than q_0, a smaller q_T can be tried until approximate equality is reached. A little experimentation will show that, unless the plan period be very short, most of the time consumption will be near the minimum; the closer initial output is to this minimum, the more will it be so. Thus the solution is a kind of soft-edge bang-bang.

Specifying a positive instead of a zero terminal growth rate, makes C_T less than q_T and means a slower growth of c and a more rapid one of q, with, of course, a lower, but still optimal, valuation of consumption. Alternatively q_T may be taken as a target, then that C_T must be found which will yield the target from the initial

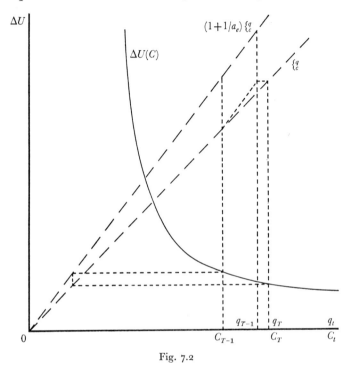

Fig. 7.2

output. It may not be feasible within the given plan time, but if this be expanded sufficiently, any target can become possible. Again, assuming feasibility, C_T may be taken as target and the calculation of C_t follows straight off and the behaviour of q_t is determined. The longer is the plan period the higher can the initial consumption be.

As an example, suppose there is given an intertemporal preference system roughly like that of fig. 7.1. Initial output, say 18, is little larger than the minimum consumption of 16. The aim is to make an optimal transition to full employment which, with the chosen technique, requires a doubling of output to 36. In order to make a smooth transition to the next phase, it is required to have a terminal rate of 2 %. With an equipment–output ratio of 4, this means a consumption, in the terminal year of 33·1. Given the marginal utility of consumption, the behaviour of consumption over any span of time can be calculated and is given in Table 7.1.

Table 7.1

	c	q	Δq	$\dfrac{\%}{\Delta q/q}$
T	33·1	36·0	1·0	2·9
$T-1$	31·0	35·0	1·5	4·5
$T-2$	27·6	33·5	1·9	6·0
$T-3$	24·2	31·6	1·9	6·4
$T-4$	22·0	29·7	2·0	7·2
$T-5$	19·4	27·7	2·1	8·2
$T-6$	17·4	25·6	1·8	7·6
$T-7$	16·5	23·8	1·5	6·7
$T-8$	16·3	22·3	1·3	6·2
$T-9$	16·2	21·0	1·0	5·0
$T-10$	16·2	20·0	0·8	4·2
$T-11$	16·1	19·2	0·6	3·2
$T-12$	16·08	18·6	0·5	2·8
0	16·05	18·1	—	—

Once consumption and terminal output are known it is easy, by recursion, to find output for each year. The transition time, T, is left open and is determined when output reduces to the initial capacity output of 18. In this case it is found to be 13 years. By putting consumption low and holding it there output is rapidly accelerated. Then as the terminal date is approached consumption is allowed to rise decelerating the growth rate to the required 2 % in $T+1$. What is striking is how different optimal growth is from the steady, constant rate in a golden age regime. The example is, admittedly, an extreme one chosen to exhibit rapid acceleration and deceleration, but qualitatively similar results will be found in less extreme cases. This fact has important consequences for the structure and composition of output as well as the scale. To keep matters simple, consider only net output and suppose consumption involves no durable output. The time path of the output vector is shown in fig. 7.3. In golden age growth is would lie on a single ray.

In principal the plan period T can be made indefinitely long thus obviating the awkwardness of an illogical transition to the behaviour in subsequent years. However, this example cannot be indefinitely extended because the problem of labour supply would sooner or later arise so long as a fixed technique is employed. Also certain complications arise in infinite programmes, as is strikingly exemplified by an infinite bang-bang, which purports to say that the best consumption programme is never actually to consume.

Technical progress and labour force growth likewise can be introduced. Technical progress eases the accumulation problem by increasing its effectiveness, thus allowing a less spartan programme

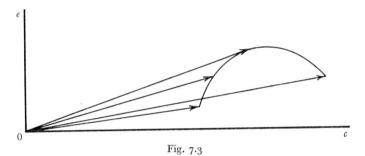

Fig. 7.3

for the early years. Population growth on the other hand makes the task harder by requiring more accumulation and/or more growth in consumption to achieve the same standard of average consumption.

7.2. *Optimal accumulation with full employment*

The problem changes character in the case of full employment of labour for then there are two limits to output so that accumulation is no longer the sole determinant of output. Suppose an industrialized economy, but one using a technique well below that which gives maximum output per head, e.g. the U.K. compared with the U.S. The labour force is constant and always fully employed.

There are a continuous set of techniques a which give outputs, q, according to the stock of e, as in fig. 7.4. The initial stock of equipment is e_0 and output q_0 and the problem is to proceed optimally to e^* q^*. It has been customary to say that as e increases to e^*, q rises along the curve to q^*, but the correctness of this has been successfully called into question. The issue is this: if e increases from e_0 to e_1 does q increase to q_1 and the answer is, in general, no. If equipment were homogeneous and interchangeable in all uses, then all the equipment old and new, would be used in the new process and the result follows. In reality a large part, but not all, of equipment is specific to its process or product and is not convertible to new uses. Depreciation allowances and disappearance through wear and tear allow some part of existing equipment to reappear in the proper form for the new processes. This only holds if the value of the output of the old equipment is unaffected by the new processes, but actually the old equipment is frequently rendered partially or wholly valueless by the new processes. The other extreme is permanently durable equipment totally specific to its technique. Reality seems to consist of both types but is probably closer to the inconvertible case. If, for simplicity, only one type is considered, it seems better to assume complete inconvertibility.

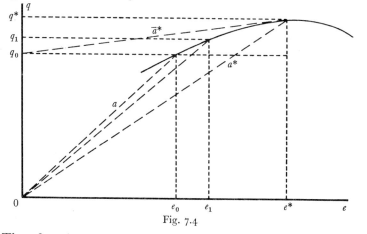

Fig. 7.4

Therefore the transition will not be made in a series of small steps to new techniques, but rather the best technique a^* will be chosen and all accumulation embodied in this form. When new equipment is rendered superfluous in order to release labour to man the new equipment, with the result that the net gain is much smaller than the productivity of the new technique by itself. The ratios are constant throughout the process and can be read off from the diagram. If there were e^* added equipment, this would require the whole labour force and add q^* to output, but it would destroy the value of all existing equipment and reduce output by q_0; so that the constant marginal product of new equipment will be $(q^* - q_0)/e^*$. In other words the net marginal productivity of new equipment is only equal the difference between its productivity and that of existing equipment. Net productivity being constant marginal and average are equal; it could be called differential productivity and denoted by $1/\bar{a}^*$.

Thus the problem, properly reinterpreted, becomes again the same as that of section 7.1.

$$(1 + 1/\bar{a}^*)q_t = q_{t+1} + (1/\bar{a}^*)C_t.$$

There are two other differences. Since this is the end of the line, no further increases being possible, terminal consumption must equal terminal output. Initial output will be much above any sort of subsistence level though it may not be much above a politically acceptable minimum consumption. The problem is to be solved exactly as before by backward recursion, with

$$q_T = q^* = C_T.$$

As in fig. 7.2, from C_T, C_{T-1} is found and this with q_T determines q_{T-1}. From C_{T-1} comes C_{T-2} which, with q_{T-1}, yields q_{T-2}, and so on until, approximately, q_{T-T} equals the given q_0. This determines T, C_0, and the optimal transition values of q_t and C_t. Such a procedure fixes the consumption so as to maximize its valuation over the period $t = 0$ to $t = T$, but it cannot do so for the wider period extending into the indefinite future, since the progression C_{T-1} to $C_T = C_{T+1} = \ldots$ is not optimal.

This awkwardness disappears if existing equipment is assumed to be homogeneous and non-specific, so that each period it can be switched to a new technique and added to the new equipment. For then $1/a_e$ gradually becomes zero as e accumulates, which means that the increments to consumption decrease to zero as q^* is approached and the process lasts indefinitely long. If a realistic compromise is adopted whereby some portion of equipment can be converted each period, through wear and tear, to new forms, then, if the process is not too rapid, the old equipment becomes transferable. Then as q approaches q^*, $\Delta q/\Delta e$ also becomes zero as $1/a_e$ become zero. As $1/a_e$ gets ever smaller, the required optimal decline in utility gets smaller and so, hence, does the required increase in consumption. As consumption comes to rest, it must do so not at a value less than q^* or greater, for both of these represent most unoptimal behaviours, in the one case, useless equipment is for ever stockpiled and in the other output declines at an accelerating pace. Unfortunately we cannot work backward from the terminal consumption for to do so requires an infinite number of steps. There is no alternative but to make a guess at

C_0 and see whether it approaches q^* as its terminal value. Then correcting up or down, a reasonably good approximation can be used initially, and, as the terminal value is approached small corrections will ensure that consumption slides into its correct final value.

The long process of industrializing an under-developed country may be conveniently divided into three distinct phases. The first consists of optimal accumulation of new equipment so as to employ the unemployed; this may take rather a long time because the high productivity equipment offers little employment, since that is its desirable characteristic. Secondly, there will be the phase of swapping the old equipment as labour is reallocated to the newer processes. The optimal initial relation of consumption to output for this phase, specifies the terminal conditions for the first phase. The third phase will consist of the slow shift from the best growth technique to that one which gives maximum consumption. Here the terminal condition is $C = q$, so that the initial conditions are determined, these in turn setting the terminal conditions for the second phase.

7.3. The evolution of the labour force

In the past population, like Topsy, just grew, and, indeed, has been so treated in this book. Yet it should be recognized that, from the time that modern medicine began seriously to reduce the death rate, such a control would sooner or later have to be accompanied by one over the birth rate, else the system could be set on a disaster course of a type observed some times in animal populations. That this ominous possibility has been so long obscured is due to the fact that the growth of populations has been associated with—whether as cause or effect is a disputed issue— an extraordinary and prolonged rise in productivity which has masked the independent effects of growing populations. What can scarcely be disputed is, however, that the misery and squalor of the early stages of industrialization were accentuated by the swelling labour force, and that it explains the very long delay before any of those prodigious technical innovations brought any comfort to the common people who actually carried them out.

Men have quite successfully controlled not only the quantity but even the quality (in so far as they knew how) of their domestic animal populations. It is, however, a problem of an altogether different order of magnitude for man to control himself not only quantitatively but even genetically. The question of norms and values arises—for whom and for what. The controller is not given with his set of values, but is himself the object of control. The wider genetic problem is awesome and, happily, is quite outside the scope of this discussion. The quantitative control of population and labour force is much simpler as well as being immediate, pressing and unavoidable.

Demographic description and control is immensely complicated and in the case of control, largely unexplored. To exhibit some of the main issues unobscured by this detail, violent over-simplification is necessary, which rules out any direct usefulness of the conclusions. The age structure is ignored as well as the very long lag between birth and addition to labour force. Men will be assumed to be born fully fledged labourers and die on leaving the labour force but are mysteriously supplied with an average number of dependents. Thus population is strictly proportional to labour force and the distinction may be ignored. Crude birth, b, and death, d, rates per capita are the sole variables to be considered, so that labour supply, l_s, is governed by

$$\Delta l_s / l_s = b - d.$$

Both d and b can be control variables, but in most cases ethical beliefs rule out intentional withdrawal of medical service to raise the death rate, even though societies readily tolerate economic policies which have the same effect. Hence d will be taken as a state variable depending solely on the average level of consumption, given the state of medical practice. The birth rate is taken to be determined by some complex set of historical, social and economic factors, but to be capable of a moderate degree of control through the taxes and subsidies, if any, which affect birth rates, and through subsidized provision of contraception and the propaganda required to encourage its use. Thus birth (and childhood) can be made more or less expensive and the means to avoid it also. There seems little doubt that if there is the will to do so, the birth rate can be appreciably altered. Whether the ethical beliefs of a country permit it is another matter. What one can say is that any nation is in for trouble which has that peculiar set of beliefs to the effect that death must always be avoided if possible and that birth must never be so.

7.4. *Malthus brought up to date*

Suppose an under-developed economy with the following characteristics: a given technique of production; rentiers who get the surplus and accumulate some fraction (usually small) of it, but whose numbers, though not their incomes, are small; a fixed, historically given, real wage w; a given birth rate, b; a death rate, d, which is a given function of the average standard of living, taken as the ratio of the wage bill, wl_d, to the labour force, l_s. Output equals total profits plus wages; a portion, σ, of profits is accumulated as net new equipment, which is always fully employed. The productivity of labour is $1/a_l$ and of equipment is $1/a_e$, so that

$$q = \frac{a_e}{\sigma}\Delta q + wa_l q,$$

or

$$g = \Delta q/q = \sigma/a_e\,(1 - wa_l).$$

Approximately (ignoring a time lag)

$$\frac{\Delta\{(l_d/l_s)w\}}{(l_d/l_s)\,w} = \frac{\Delta wl_d}{wl_d} - \Delta l_s/l_s.$$

Since the wage bill is a constant proportion of output, it has the same growth rate. The uncontrolled dynamics of the system are then completely determined as shown in fig. 7.5. Stationary equilibrium may be defined as an unchanged standard of living with the growth rate of labour force equal to the of the wage bill, i.e. $g = \Delta l_s/l_s$. Since $\Delta l_s/l_s = b - d(wl_d/l_s)$ it can be plotted easily. The equilibrium standard of living is at E; it is stable. If $\Delta l_s/l_s$ is below the growth rate of output, employment grows faster than work force so that l_d/l_s increases, raising the average standard of living, lowering the death rate and accelerating l_s relative to l_d. For values above E the converse holds, so that the system is stable. The system must lie to the left of the point F where there is full employment with $l_d = l_s$ and the wage equals the average standard of living. The equilibrium is achieved by inducing that

181

rate of unemployment (more or less disguised) EF/oE, which will so impoverish the populace that it grows no faster than employment.

Suppose that there is a coup, and that the first action of the new government is to enforce a general rise in the real wage. To see what happens it is helpful to rephrase the system as follows: call the average standard of living

$$z = (l_d/l_s)w$$

with
$$\frac{\Delta z}{z} = \frac{\Delta w}{w} + \frac{\Delta l_d}{l_d} - \frac{\Delta l_s}{l_s} = g - \Delta l_s/l_s,$$

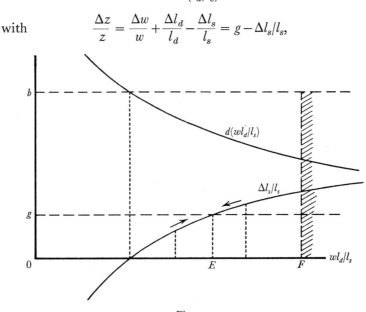

Fig. 7.5

where $\Delta w/w = o$, since w is constant, and $\Delta l_d/l_d = g$; g depends on w as shown in fig. 7.6. So also does z, for a given l_d/l_s. Given w', g' is determined, and given $(l_d/l_s)_0$, λ is determined, which in turn determines $(\Delta l_s/l_s)_0$. But the difference between this value of $\Delta l_s/l_s$ and g', tells us how z must alter. The rate of employment, l_d/l_s, rises, and z moves towards z_e, the equilibrium. If, then, the new government raises the wage to w'', the standard of living rises to z_0'' and with it the popularity of the regime. But g goes down to g'' and $\Delta l_s/l_s$ goes up, i.e. the rate of creation of jobs goes down and that of the creation of job seekers goes up, so that the standard of living begins a rapid fall, slowly decelerating towards z_e''. Thus in the long run raising the wage leads to a more than proportionate fall in the employment rate, l_d/l_s, so that the standard of living of employed and unemployed, taken together, must fall. A naive approach has led to everyone being worse off, workers poorer and rentiers with a smaller share of a less rapidly growing output. A more sophisticated analysis would have revealed that, to get the

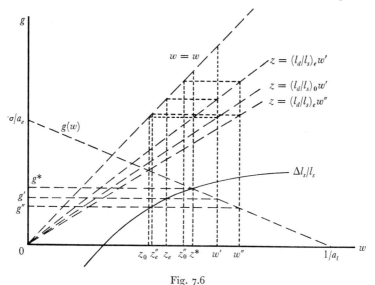

Fig. 7.6

highest standard of living and of growth rate, wages should have been lowered to z^*, at the point at which $\Delta l_s/l_s$ equals the growth rate line. Then, after an initial fall in the standard of living, it would have risen to its maximum possible value as a result of the gradual elimination of unemployment with $l_d = l_s$. This is the highest maintainable z, i.e. a Golden Rule.

7.5. A dynamic programme for population

It would not be surprising if, having raised wages and only succeeded in lowering the standard of living, the government were to be overturned again. However implausible, imagine that the extremists have correctly understood Malthus and all his dismal science. They, therefore, undertake to raise the long-run standard of living by reducing the birth rate, Such a programme requires real resources, but it also may save real resources in the form of lower family benefits, etc. Also its initial costs may be much higher than its continuing costs and a host of other complications. The principle involved can be adequately illustrated, nevertheless, by the simple assumption that the more real resources devoted to it, the greater will be the reduction of the birth rate, down to some minimum, positive level.

Such a programme of population control has a basic superiority over a policy of accumulating equipment to provide jobs for

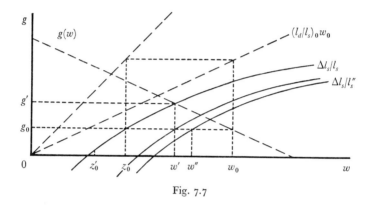

Fig. 7.7

everyone. Suppose that the prescription is a programme which will produce eventual full employment. The two types of programme are then to be compared. The economy is in a low-level equilibrium with $g_0 = \Delta l_s / l_s$ and an employment rate well short of unity, as shown in fig. 7.7. To achieve full employment by accumulation, w must be reduced to w', reducing z proportionately to z_0'. $\Delta z / z = g' - \Delta l_s / l_s$ and z rises gradually towards w', with l_d / l_s rising to unity. By contrast, if a tax is levied so as to reduce w to w'', but leaving profits and hence g unaltered, the spending of these real resources will lower the birth rate and hence shift $\Delta l_s / l_s$ downward to $\Delta l_s / l_s''$. The difference between the two depends on the quantitative relations, g being always higher with the accumulation policy. As drawn, the initial wage, the initial standard of living and the final one are all higher in the population control policy. This is because the evidence, such as it is, is that it is very much cheaper to reduce the number of jobs needed than to increase the number of jobs with their associated equipment.

The revolutionary council, having embraced a policy of reducing population growth, is free to reduce accumulation. They can force up wages, reduce profits and accumulation (only by a fraction of the reduction in profits), and then tax the increased wages to finance the population policy. The only limit is a possible floor below which the birth rate cannot be pushed or below which it can only be pushed by very large outlays. Thus suppose, in fig. 7.8 that the effective lower limit to $\Delta l_s / l_s$ is $(\Delta l_s / l_s)'$ and that this requires a reduction of wages by tax from w' to w''. The wage

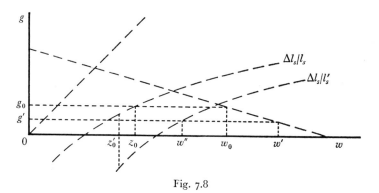

Fig. 7.8

is raised from w_0 to w', reducing g to g'. The wage after tax is reduced only from w_0 to w'' and the standard of living from z_0 to z_0'. This leads to a decrease in labour force whilst equipment continues to grow though at a reduced rate, so that unemployment is rapidly reduced from both sides. The labour force gradually ceases to decline, due to the rapid rise in z, and thereafter gradually rises towards the constant growth rate in employment and output, g'. z rises to w'', which represents the highest attainable standard of living. It seems clear that the policy of population limitation is economically superior to accumulation.

7.6. A dynamic optimal population programme

Throughout this book two elements have been singled out as presenting the most basic limit on output—equipment and labour. Nothing can be done to alter either in the short run, but equipment does change in the long run as a result of decisions and some of the problems of optimal choice have been discussed in sections 7.2 and 7.3. By contrast, population (labour force) has been treated as changing but not subject to decision. In reality it is profoundly affected by social choices in the widest sense and, no doubt, it will become more so. The problem then arises of an optimal sequence of decisions directly affecting population.

Having considered the case of optimal accumulation with constant population, we now take up optimal population with constant equipment, employment and output. An under-developed country with large unemployment produces a fixed output which is shared equally by employed and unemployed. The prescribed goal is to reach full employment of labour, $l_d/l_s = 1$, and to do so, after due reflection on the argument of section 7.5, solely by reduction of labour force rather than by creation of productive jobs by accumulation. The initial conditions are given by history, q_0 a constant, l_d also a constant, and an initial labour force, l_{s_0}. l_s is to be reduced to l_d. The population is to be reduced but this leaves open the question of how rapidly this is to be done, whether at a constant or a changing rate, and over how long a period. The decision rule is to be that the passage from initial to end-point is to be made optimal, in the light of the community's valuation over the whole period.

Especially urgent is the question of what it is, economically, that the community does value. At least two criteria have been suggested. Each individual values his own intake of goods and services and if, at this level of abstraction, all individuals are alike and have equal incomes, this is simply the value of the average standard of living, $u(z)$. For the whole community, it would seem logical to assume that the total valuation is the sum of the individual valuations or $(l_s)u(z)$. In view of the importance of the issue, it has been surprisingly little discussed. The problem is whether quantitative states of mind can be added like bushels of wheat, or whether it is like adding cows and horses. It is to be noted that we are involved in adding over time the quantified valuations of our average sensual man. Perhaps the best way to decide is in terms of the practical consequences. Would the welfare of the U.K. go up or down if it gave Northern Ireland to its Southern counterpart? If l_s is included, it must go down, and if only z is considered it must go up. It is largely a problem about whether such a question may properly be asked or answered. Or again, can we say that India is better off than Italy because, though poorer on the average, there are so many more of them?

The type of assumption made will obviously have a vital effect on optimum population policy. Purely to simplify, it is here assumed that valuation is given by $U(z)$ alone. Thus stated the problem is qualitatively the same as the optimal accumulation one, but it works out somewhat differently. By consuming less now and spending the saving on reducing the birth rate, average output becomes higher later thus making possible a higher consumption

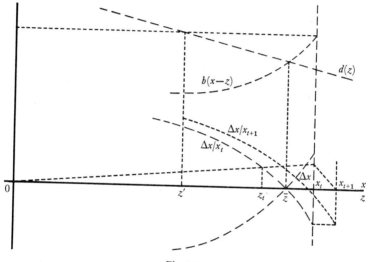

Fig. 7.9

later. The sequence of decisions about consumption must obey Ramsey's Rule to be optimal and they must conform to the conditions laid down for the programme.

Actual output, employment, and productivity are constant, but output per head of labour force, $\bar{q}/l_s = x$, will be rising as l_s decreases towards l_d. x might be called crude productivity and is a state variable. The standard of living, z, is open to choice, except that it can never be greater than x, and hence is a control variable.

$$\Delta l_s/l_s = b - d,$$

where d depends on z and b on $x - z$. Since q is constant

$$\Delta x/x = -\Delta l_s/l_s = d - b.$$

These relations are illustrated, with no attempt at realism, in fig. 7.9. A subsistence standard is z' and $\bar{z}$ would yield a stationary solution. For any given x_t, the choice of z_t sets $\Delta x/x_t$ and hence x_{t+1}. The b curve, and hence that of $\Delta x/x$, is shifted with Δx.

Dynamic optimality requires the reduction of z until the additional crude productivity thus obtained is just offset by the fall of the marginal utility of consuming such an increase of goods. This means that the rate of decrease of the marginal valuation of goods must equal the rate of increase of the output of goods (both in per capita of the labour force), thus

$$\frac{\Delta(\Delta u)}{\Delta u} = -\frac{\Delta x}{x}.$$

From this relation follow the kinematics of the system. Given x_t, the choice of a z_t, determines the growth rate to x_{t+1}. This fixes the required percentage decline in marginal utility, which in turn determines the percentage rise in z. If $\Delta z/z$ is greater than $\Delta x/x$, then z will be creeping closer to x and therefore reducing the outlay on, and hence the decline in, population. If $\Delta z/z$ is less than $\Delta x/x$, then output per capita is accelerating. In consequence, the relation between these two quantities, which is the dominant dynamic element, can be stated in terms of the elasticity of the marginal valuation curve. If it is elastic, a 5 % rate of growth in x means a 5 % fall in Δu and hence a greater than 5 % rise in z, with the result that z moves closer to x, thus reducing its rate of growth. Or, if there is unit elasticity, they grow at the same rate, maintain a constant proportion one to the other, and both slowly accelerate.

On the assumption that, as z is reduced towards a positive lower limit, its marginal utility rises without limit, the elasticity of the curve must become less than unity. Therefore if the initial x is placed near this lower limit, x accelerates away from z with the result that more and more surplus is applied to reducing population and hence accelerating x, and, in turn, z. As x advances, z advances less rapidly, and its intersection with the $\Delta x/x$ curve rises, maintaining the acceleration. If the evaluation curve remains inelastic, the system arrives at its terminal point $x = 1/a_e$, $l_d/l_s = 1$, at its maximum growth rate. However, its terminal growth rate must be zero, since full employment has been reached and no further increase is possible by reduction of unemployment. z_T is advanced to $\bar{z}$ (fig. 7.10), and the growth rate of x makes a discontinuous jump to zero.

It is almost certain that for some large value of z, the marginal valuation curve flattens out enough to become elastic. If this happens in the course of the programme, then $\Delta x/x$ becomes less than $\Delta z/z$; z begins to catch up with x; the surplus devoted to increasing x is diminished; both x and z decelerate. If, initially, the curve is elastic and remains so, then initial z must be made low enough to grow faster than z throughout and still terminate enough below x_T to ensure a constant, full employment labour force. This could mean a very low initial standard of living, but it can never require one lower than the lower limit, since this enforces a changeover to an inelastic curve.

The construction of an optimal programme proceeds as follows: x_0 is given by the labour force and the output; $\Delta x/x_T = 0$, this determines the required terminal standard of living, $z_T = \bar{z}$; it is thus necessary to find that x_{T-1}, and $\Delta x/x_{t-1}$ such that z would just rise to z_T. If the valuation curve is elastic at this point, the rate at $T-1$ might be quite small, say $\frac{1}{2}\%$, but if it is inelastic the rate might be large, say 4 or 5 %. Proceeding thus by recursion, at accelerating or decelerating growth rates depending on the elasticity, the time shape of optimal transition can be generated. When x has been decreased to the given x_0, the programme is solved, the initial standard of living is determined, along with the number of periods required for an optimal passage from initial unemployment to full employment. The growth rates are most unlikely to be constant and the most likely result is an initial acceleration and then a gradual deceleration to zero. But, depending on the circumstances, there may be continued acceleration and a sudden drop to zero, or, beginning with high growth rates, there may be deceleration throughout to the terminal zero rate.

It is not likely that any economy will ever pursue a policy based solely on this pure depopulation strategy. Particularly serious is the wildly unrealistic assumption of no lag between birth and death rates, and the growth of the labour force. The fact is there is something like a 10 to 20 years lag (and much longer still if the age composition be taken account of), and this is longer than the longest lags, e.g. for dams or steel mills, involved in accumulation. Because of this, and for other reasons, the hypothetical superiority of population policy over accumulation policy is not so clear in reality. Therefore what is required is an optimal analysis combining the two policies and taking account of the average lags involved. It is necessary to take full account of the heavier outlays of accumulation in contrast with the cheaper but more slowly maturing results of population control. The resulting complications rule out any further discussion of the problem here.

APPENDIX

MATHEMATICAL FORMULATION OF
THE MODEL

There are many excellent mathematical treatments of linear economic models, to which the reader with the appropriate equipment is referred. It may, however, be helpful to indicate how some of the variants of this particular model may be set up. The great power of linearity only really becomes apparent when the confines of two dimensions are cast off.

There are m processes and n goods, including labour, with $m > n$. The outputs from the m processes are an m element column vector $\{x\}$ these being separated into groups or sectors, giving identical outputs in an n element vector $\{q\}$. The technology is specified by an n by m rectangular matrix $[\,a\,]$. The prices of the n goods are $\langle p \rangle$; repeating these as many times as there are processes for each good, gives an m element row vector for process prices, $\langle \rho \rangle$. All prices and quantities are non-negative. Inputs must be less than or equal to outputs available from the previous period, thus

$$(1+g)[\,a\,]\{x_t\} \leqslant \{g_t\}.$$

In equilibrium cost including interest should never be below price, thus

$$\langle p \rangle(1+\pi)[\,a\,] \geqslant \langle \rho \rangle.$$

These inequalities may be turned into equalities by introducing the 'slack' variables, profit per unit, $\langle \pi \rangle$, and additions to stock (excess supply), $\{\Delta s\}$. The problem is to maximize $\langle p \rangle\{q\}$, subject to the first set of inequalities and to minimize $\langle \rho \rangle\{x\}$ subject to the second set. Adding slack variables, premultiply the first by p, giving

$$\langle p \rangle(1+g)[\,a\,]\{x\} + \langle p \rangle\{\Delta s\} = \langle p \rangle\{q\}$$

and postmultiply the second by $\{x\}$, so that

$$\langle p \rangle(1+\pi)[\,a\,]\{x\} + \langle \Pi \rangle\{x\} = \langle \rho \rangle\{x\}.$$

For the moment suppose $\pi = g$ is given; by definition $\langle \Pi \rangle \leqslant 0$, and $\{\Delta s\} \geqslant 0$. If, when $\Pi_i < 0$, x_i is set at zero then $\langle \Pi \rangle \{x\} = 0$, and if, when $\Delta s_i > 0$, p_i is set at zero, when $\langle p \rangle \{\Delta s\} = 0$. Therefore

$$\langle p \rangle \{q\} = \langle p \rangle (1 + g)[a]\{x\} = \langle \rho \rangle \{x\},$$

so that we get a minimum–maximum with the two scalar quantities equal. If $\rho \cdot x$ could be made smaller, $p \cdot q$ would cease to be a maximum, and if $p \cdot q$ could be made larger $\rho \cdot x$ would no longer be minimal. If the two quantities are equal, then the twin conditions above follow, so that they are necessary and sufficient conditions. Barring special cases, this chooses one optimal technique for each good; it also chooses which goods not to produce in the cases in which all Π_i are negative. It also shows that $\pi = g$ since

$$1 + g = \frac{p \cdot q}{pax} = \frac{\rho x}{pax} = 1 + \pi.$$

Neither π nor g is given and they are in fact determined by the same operation. Start with large π so that all costs are greater than their prices; reduce π, altering prices, until, for all goods produced, just one process gives a cost, with profit, equal to its price, with all other processes for each good having cost greater than price. This determines simultaneously all prices, all techniques to be used and the minimum profit rate. Next take a small growth rate such that inputs (with growth) do not exhaust the outputs. Then, increasing the common growth rate and suitably altering outputs, find the values for which operating just one process per good uses all the output of each, such that the use of any other processes would require inputs greater than the outputs. This chooses outputs, greatest growth rate, and, by means of zero outputs for most processes, the best techniques of production. Since the twin conditions imply

$$1 + \pi^* = \langle \rho^* \rangle \{x^*\} / \langle p^* \rangle [a]\{x^*\}$$
$$= \langle p^* \rangle \{q^*\} / \langle p^* \rangle [a]\{x^*\} = 1 + g^*$$

it follows that the minimum π equals the maximum g.

For a viable economy the greatest eigenvalue π^* and its associated eigenray p^* may be located easily in principle even if not in practice. Start with an arbitrary $p(0)$, and find the profit (or loss) with each technique, thus

$$\langle p(0) \rangle \left[\overline{| 1 + \pi |} [a] \right] = \langle \rho(0) \rangle,$$

where $\overline{|1+\pi|}$ is a rectangular diagonal matrix with a profit rate repeated on each line as many times as there are processes. For each good there will be a greatest profit rate. Taking any value, π_0, between the greatest and least of these, and using for each good only the technique with the greatest profit rate, obtain a first approximation

$$\langle p(0)\rangle[(1+\pi_0)[\,a\,]] = \langle p(0)\rangle.$$

Then repeat the process, calculating profit rates from

$$\langle p(1)\rangle[\overline{|1+\pi|}[\,a\,]] = \langle \rho(1)\rangle,$$

obtaining a second estimate, π_1, and, using it as a common mark-up, find a second approximation to the eigenvector of prices.

$$\langle p(1)\rangle[(1+\pi_1)[\,a\,]] = \langle p(2)\rangle,$$

and so on until, approximately,

$$\langle p(n)\rangle[(1+\pi)][a] = \langle p(n)\rangle.$$

This selects p^* and a square a^*.

Because row and column eigenvalues are the same, there is no need to repeat the process for the dual problem. There exists a q^* for which

$$(1+\pi^*)a^*q^* = q^*,$$

and the only problem is to find it. With any arbitrary output vector calculate a first approximation, a second and so on.

$$(1+\pi^*)a^*q(0) = q(1)$$
$$(1+\pi^*)^2a^{*2}q(0) = q(2)$$
$$\vdots \qquad\qquad \vdots$$
$$(1+\pi^*)^n a^{*n}q(0) = q(n)$$

That this process converges to the output eigenray, can be seen as follows:

$$q(n+1)^-q(n) = (1+\pi^*)^{n+1}a^{*n+1}q(0) - (1+\pi^*)^n a^{*n}q(0).$$

When a matrix is raised to a high power, all its elements grow or decline from step to step in the proportion of its largest, or dominant, eigenvalue, i.e. $(1+r^*)a^{*n+1} = a^{*n}$. This means that $q(n+1) = q(n)$ and hence they are the desired eigenvector.

The von Neumann type analysis given above is appropriate only to equilibrium and should not be used to investigate disequilibrium situations. There are five broad types of dynamic-adjustment listed in 2.3–price-cost discrepancy leading to price change, suitable for the analysis of wage-price spiralling; output demand inequalities leading to output adjustment, as analysed in the behaviour of inventories; Walrasian excess supply leading to price change; Marshallian abnormal profit leading to output evolution; and finally, cross-field dynamics, which are at once the most interesting and the most difficult to analyse.

The long-run dynamics of the system are known; there must be eigenoutputs and eigenprices with a single uniform profit-growth rate. However, in a system subject to continual and sometimes violent outside disturbances, the short-run outputs and prices will certainly diverge from these eigenvector values.

First consider the case of mark-up price determination, in the short-run, with an unchanging, square technology, and with a mark-up established and equal to the greatest eigenvalue. Given initial disequilibrium prices and no further disturbances, prices will be set by the standard mark-up, $1 + r^*$.

$$p(0)(1 + r^*)a^* = p(1)$$
$$p(1)(1 + r^*)a^* = p(2) = p(0)(1 + r^*)^2 a^{*2}$$
$$\vdots \qquad \qquad \vdots$$
$$p(0)(1 + r^*)a^{*t} = p(t)$$

$(1 + r^*)^t$ increases but a^{*t} decreases, so what happens to $p(t)$? By virtue of the behaviour of a matrix raised to a high power, we see that $p(t) \to p(t+1)$ and hence $p(t) \to p^*$ as $t \to \infty$. It is also evident that the iterative search for a solution is under these conditions an exact analogue of certain dynamic market processes, and that likewise dynamic stability and convergence to a solution are analogues and are both assured by viability. In this simple model the more viable (productive) the economy the more stable and the more rapid the convergence.

To do the symmetrical analysis for output, it is convenient to reverse the von Neumann scheme. In the current period each sector experiences a demand a^*q, and they all expect a normal growth rate of $g^* = r^*$, setting output in the next period equal to expected demand, so that

$$q(t+1) = (1 + g^*)a^*q(t).$$

For large t approximately

$$q(t+1) = (1+g^*)^{t+1} a^{*t+1} q(0) = (1+g^*)^t a^{*t} q(0) = q(t)$$
$$= q^*.$$

Throughout it is necessary to assume that the system is 'indecomposable', that is to say no sector or group of sectors is entirely independent, directly or indirectly, of all other sectors. The consequence of this is that no sector can be for long out of step with the others. Various types of cross-field dynamics are particularly illuminating on the processes by which disequilibrium may be eliminated. Thus if a sector grows more slowly than the others, they will run down the stocks of its output, so that there will be an upward pressure on its relative price. The rise in its price will raise profits and accelerate growth until it is in step with the others. The opposite will happen for too rapid a growth. Basically the type of relation is

$$\Delta q = p(I-a),$$
$$\Delta p = -(I-a)q,$$

or better, in dimensionless form,

$$\Delta q/q = \langle 1 \rangle (I - pap^{-1}),$$
$$\Delta p/p = -(I - q^{-1}aq)\{1\}.$$

Even though both of these are too simple for adequate understanding, their analysis is too complicated to be pursued in this brief note.

The foregoing has constituted a rather exceptional form of linear programming in that it is homogeneous, so that scale is completely indeterminate: output can be at any level and proceed to grow forever at a constant exponential rate. The more usual type has a pair of given vectors which determine the scale. Excluding labour from the list of goods, the model may be rephrased in a more usual form.

Maximize $\qquad\langle p \rangle\{c\}$

subject to $\qquad\langle p \rangle[\,I-a\,] \leqslant w \langle a_l \rangle,$

and minimize $\qquad w\langle a_l \rangle\{x\}$

subject to $\qquad[\,I-a\,]\{x\} \geqslant \{c\},$

where c is net product or 'final bill of goods'. In the simplest case it is consumption but it may be sophisticated to include investment, government use, and exports. The technology a is given along with c, a_l, and w; p and x vectors have to be found which give a min-max or saddle-point. The n elements of p and c define the dimensions of the space, which will be spanned by any n independent vectors from among the m columns of $[I-a]$. A solution consists principally in finding, amongst the many sets of n basis vectors, the optimal set. The dot product of any p with any column (technique) of $[I-a]$ gives the surplus available to pay wages (profits taken as zero). By various methods of search, it is possible to find a set of prices which give for each of the n goods just one technique which yields enough to pay the wage cost, with all other processes unable to produce enough to cover wage costs. It is then impossible to raise any prices further and hence this will maximize the value of aggregate net output. Indeed, by virtue of the Samuelson Substitution Theorem, it will maximize not only the given c but any net output whatsoever. There is, then, in the normal case, an optimal basis of n techniques, with which is associated an optimal eigenvector

$$\langle p^* \rangle = w \langle a_i^* \rangle (I - a^*)^{-1},$$

where a^* is an n by n square matrix consisting of the optimal basis vectors. Given the money wage, the price level is determined but will vary proportionately with w, so that what is really determined is the real wage, the price level and the money wage being completely arbitrary, and unimportant.

For all other techniques, which have a surplus less than the wage cost, the output, x_i, is zero. For the n non-zero outputs, begin with large values and then gradually reduce them until gross output less inputs just equals the required net output in each case. They can be lowered no more; the zero outputs are also minimal (negative outputs are excluded), so that these values minimize the aggregate wage cost (and employment), with the inequality signs turning to equalities. Once the optimal basis has been chosen, however, it is not necessary to go through the search a second time for the dual; simply solve the n equations

$$q = (I - a^*)^{-1} c.$$

Premultiply the output equation by p and postmultiply the price equation by x; this reduces the dual sets of constraints to a single pair of scalar inequalities,

$$\langle p \rangle \{c\} \leqslant \langle p \rangle [\, I - a\,]\{x\} \leqslant w \langle a_l \rangle \{x\}.$$

By virtue of the zeros in x^* the solution becomes a pair of equalities. Therefore the minimal wage cost equals the value of net output, i.e. aggregate factor payments equal the value of aggregate net product. The given c determines x (or dropping zeros, q), but this is a relatively unsatisfactory formulation, for, unlike a_l, c is not really given and unalterable. What may be given is the total labour supply, L, so that the real limiting inequality is $\langle a_l \rangle \{x\} \leqslant L$. By increasing c in, possibly variable, proportion, x can be increased until the inequality becomes an equality. If c is such that $a_1 . x > L$, there is no feasible solution.

In this way, given a pattern of consumption, the solution produces the greatest satisfaction of wants consistent with the given technology and the given unproduced inputs. It is inhomogeneous and hence limited to a given scale indefinitely. However, nothing essential in the argument would have been altered, had we been given $(1 + g)\, a$ and $(1 + r)\, a$ instead of a. This is the Golden Rule, which maximizes consumption subject to a required growth rate. With full employment the growth rate is set by the growth rate of the labour force. The scale again becomes indefinite with c increasing at a rate g, so that, since consumption is maximized at each point of time, it is maximized over a time span of any length.

Consumption is maximized subject to a constant growth rate in output. But is this desirable or optimal? Thus take the problem of VII.1, where output is limited, not by employment, but by last period's output, i.e.

$$q_{t-1} - aq_t \geqslant c_t.$$

This can be represented by a partitioned matrix in which the entries are the matrices for each year, thus, for example,

$$\begin{bmatrix} 1 & -a & 0 & 0 \\ 0 & 1 & -a & 0 \\ 0 & 0 & 1 & -a \end{bmatrix} \begin{Bmatrix} q_0 \\ q_1 \\ q_2 \\ q_3 \end{Bmatrix} \geqslant \begin{Bmatrix} C_1 \\ C_2 \\ C_3 \end{Bmatrix}$$

a nearly diagonal block matrix. The same goods in different years are considered to be distinct, with a corresponding increase in variables, constraints and degrees of freedom. Here we do not have c given and solve for q, but the reverse (along with initial and terminal conditions). Given a social valuation v for each good in each year, the problem becomes one of maximizing $v.c$ over the entire time span. Or if there is an unchanged utility function applicable to consumption regardless of dating $1.u(c)$ can be maximized. This becomes a very complicated calculation, but it may be possible to simplify it somewhat if c_t can be treated as $\gamma_t\ \bar{c} + \bar{b}$, so that it is only necessary to maximize a linear combination of scalars instead of vectors. Whatever the solution, it is most unlikely to be one with a constant growth rate.

Given a min-max solution, with $\pi = g$ specified, of

$$p(I - (1+g)a) \leqslant (1+g)wa_l,$$

and
$$(I - (1+g)a)x \geqslant c$$

it is evident that there is a basic difference between changes in g and in w. Changes in w merely alter the scale of p, leaving structure and hence solution the same, whereas a change in g is one in the structure and alters everything. A rise in g means a change in relative prices but more especially a rise in price level, hence a fall in the real wage. Consumption is unaltered but output and employment must rise with a fall in consumption per head.

A solution means the following equalities hold:

$$p^*(I - a^*) = g(p^*a^* + wa_l) + wa_l,$$
$$(I - a^*)q^* = ga^*q^* + c.$$

Postmultiply the first by q^* and premultiply the second by p^*, thus establishing the equality of factor incomes with the value of net output. This form is suitable for a number of applied problems. By holding prices constant, the theory of output and employment can be studied; by holding output constant, the theory of prices can be investigated; with some complications both can be allowed to vary. To pursue these analyses, it is necessary to specify the determinants of π, g, w, and c. Further complications can be followed by introducing taxes, government expenditure, exports and imports.

INDEX

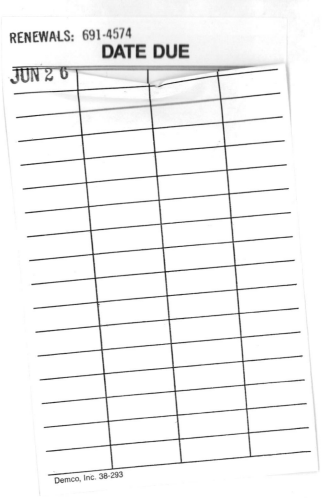

RENEWALS: 691-4574

DATE DUE

JUN 2 6

Demco, Inc. 38-293